Saying It Right
Tools for Deft Leadership

Michael B. Gilbert

ROWMAN & LITTLEFIELD
Lanham • Boulder • New York • London

Published by Rowman & Littlefield
A wholly owned subsidiary of The Rowman & Littlefield Publishing Group, Inc.
4501 Forbes Boulevard, Suite 200, Lanham, Maryland 20706
www.rowman.com

6 Tinworth Street, London SE11 5AL, United Kingdom

Copyright © 2020 by Michael B. Gilbert

All rights reserved. No part of this book may be reproduced in any form or by any electronic or mechanical means, including information storage and retrieval systems, without written permission from the publisher, except by a reviewer who may quote passages in a review.

British Library Cataloguing in Publication Information Available

Library of Congress Cataloging-in-Publication Data

Names: Gilbert, Michael B., 1944- author.
Title: Saying it right : tools for deft leadership / Michael B. Gilbert.
Description: Lanham : Rowman & Littlefield, [2020] | Includes bibliographical references.
Identifiers: LCCN 2019049321 (print) | LCCN 2019049322 (ebook) | ISBN 9781475856118 (cloth) | ISBN 9781475856125 (paperback) | ISBN 9781475856132 (epub)
Subjects: LCSH: Communication in management. | Communication in organizations. | Leadership.
Classification: LCC HD30.3 .G528 2020 (print) | LCC HD30.3 (ebook) | DDC 658.4/5--dc23
LC record available at https://lccn.loc.gov/2019049321
LC ebook record available at https://lccn.loc.gov/2019049322

This book is dedicated to my grandchildren.
You are the hope of a better world.

Contents

List of Tables	ix
List of Figures	xi
Foreword by Dr. Taibi Kahler	xiii
Acknowledgments	xv
Prologue	xvii

SECTION I: RAW MATERIALS: LEADERSHIP CONCEPTS   1

1 The Beginning Stage	3
Communicate to Succeed	4
Audiences to Consider	5
Moving Ahead	6
Effective Leadership	6
Standards	10
Gender Myths and Realities	11
A Vision for the Future	12
2 Chaos: The Wrinkling of Order and Logic	15
Parental Administration	15
Chaos	17
Re-Establishing Stability	18
3 The Start of Communication	21
Listening	21
Listening to Communicate	23
Keys to Effective Listening	27

4	Communication Blueprints: Different Tools for Different Builders	33
	Personality Models	33
	An Overview of Process Communication	37
	The PCM in Action	38
	Motivation	42
	Interaction Styles	45
	Day-to-Day Operations	45
	Benefits	47
	Conclusion	47
	Who Am I?	47
	What's to Come	50

SECTION II: BUILDING BLOCKS: PURE PERSONALITY TYPES — 51

5	Pure Harmonizer: Barbara	53
	Profile	56
	Problem Situation	56
6	Pure Thinker: Alfred	59
	Profile	62
	Problem Situation	62
7	Pure Persister: Matthew	65
	Profile	67
	Problem Situation	68
8	Pure Imaginer: Dorothy	71
	Profile	74
	Problem Situation	74
9	Pure Rebel: Angie	77
	Profile	80
	Problem Situation	80
10	Pure Promoter: Doug	83
	Profile	87
	Problem Situation	87

SECTION III: PUTTING THINGS TOGETHER: BUILDING EFFECTIVE COMMUNICATION SKILLS — 89

11	Dealing with Conflict	91
	Preparation	91

	Managing Conflict	92
	Resolving Conflict Integratively	96
12	Solving Problems Cooperatively: A Blueprint for Success	99
	Diagnosing	101
	Adapting	107
	Communicating	110
13	Changing Leadership Behavior	119
	Changing Behavior	119
	Reinforcing Training	121

Epilogue: Installing the Capstones	123
Appendix A: Frames of Preference	133
Appendix B: Dealing with Distress: Suggestions for Responses to Behaviors	141
About the Author	145

Tables

Table 3.1.	Communication Skills Learning	22
Table 3.2.	Administrators' Listening Behaviors Perceptions	25
Table 3.3.	Staff Perceptions of Administrators' Listening	26
Table 4.1.	Comparative Personality Indicators	35
Table 4.2.	Interaction Styles	46
Table 12.1.	Distress Patterns, Conflict Style, & Masks	103
Table 12.2.	Establishing Priorities	109
Table 12.3.	Choosing Among Alternatives	109
Table 12.4.	Communication Preferences	110
Table 12.5.	Personality, Word Choices, & Communication Channels	112
Table 12.6.	Frames of Preference	115

Figures

Figure 3.1. Communication Rainbow 23
Figure 4.1. Sample Base 36
Figure 4.2. Sample Phase 44
Figure 12.1. Sample Phase 101
Figure Epilogue.1. Assessing Matrix 124

Foreword

Leadership literally means forging new paths with colleagues. That's what Dr. Michael Gilbert does so masterfully in this book. He walks with the reader, giving step-by-step suggestions to managers and leaders in how to connect, motivate, and resolve conflict throughout their administrative responsibilities. Dr. Gilbert shares the secrets of how to communicate with all types of colleagues, including how to talk each one's language (perception), how to motivate each one individually (psychological need), and how to resolve conflicts easily and effectively.

Dr. Gilbert is an expert in the Process Communication Model® (PCM), attaining Master Trainer status. PCM profiles, seminars, and books have applied in business, management, sales, teams, mentoring, parenting, health fields, religion, politics, and in education for more than 30 years, touching the lives of more than 1,000,000 people, in dozens of countries.

With a solid foundation of research (including many dissertations), the Process Communication Model® (PCM) is one of the most significant contributions to leadership. Former President Bill Clinton publicly acclaimed that this model of communicating "is a great contribution . . ."

I am lucky to have discovered the fabric of processes that holds together the contents of how we communicate. I am fortunate to have such a friend and colleague, Dr. Michael Gilbert, who has devoted his life to educating leaders, in education and other organizations.

Michael's examples of real-life problems and solutions, insights into behaviors, plans for success, and integrations of classic approaches are as appealing to the seasoned leader as they are to those just beginning their careers. With respect and pride, I pass the torch to Dr. Michael Gilbert in leadership. With his vast experience, myriad professional accomplishments, and expansive knowledge, Michael, I believe, will help light the way of achieving our PCM mission: to improve the quality of professional and personal life and performance.

Taibi Kahler

Taibi Kahler is a clinical psychologist and organizational consultant. He is the creator of the Process Communication Model, which underpins this book.

—MBG

Acknowledgments

I am indebted to my colleague and friend, Taibi Kahler for his generous guidance and mentoring of me in my understanding of his prodigious and comprehensive Process Communication Model (PCM), and for his kind comments in the Foreword.

I appreciate the work of Dr. Nandini Daljit, a Canadian eduator, for her foresight in acknowledging that dealing with chaos is a critical concept in organizational effectiveness.

I thank the myriad of professionals who have been my students and who have become my colleagues—for the honor of working with them and for what they have taught me. I have grown getting to know and interacting with the worldwide network of PCM trainers. I am a better person for having known and worked with all of these people.

Michael Gilbert

Prologue

Did you pause for a moment when you read the title? Did you think, "What is saying it wrong?"

What we have learned is that *how* you say something is as important as *what* you say (Kahler, 2010). It might be even more important. This book is retooled from my earlier work, *Communicating Effectively: Tools for Educational Leaders* (Gilbert, 2012).

When I considered the overarching theme of leadership, I thought I might write something broader for those who are leaders or who aspire to be leaders.

The field of leadership is replete with books that deal with the technical, conceptual, and human concepts related to organizational programs and personnel. This book focuses on the critical underpinning of human interaction —communication.

There is a story (or maybe a fable) that periodically circulates through organizations:

> It seems that an employee with a problem walks into a meeting with his supervisor. As he enters the meeting and either because the supervisor knows the purpose of the meeting or picks up some nonverbal cues, he says, "I see you've brought *your* monkey with you. (Of course, he is alluding to the colleague's problem.)
>
> "We will take as much time as we need to talk about your monkey. You can tell me whatever you think I need to know about your monkey. We will examine your monkey up one side and down the other. We will give your monkey whatever attention you think it needs, but when we are finished, knowing that it is your monkey, you will take your monkey with you."

We know that people want to avoid conflict. For most, conflict is uncomfortable. When we need to confront the incompatibilities we see between us and others, we would prefer many times that someone else deal with the problem. So we want them to take care of our "monkey."

The issue is how to communicate effectively in order to resolve conflict and solve problems. The operative word is *effective.*

There are many who can do the job (that is, they are efficient), but fewer who can do the job right (that is, be effective). Maybe this is also the distinction to be made between management and leadership (Bennis & Nanus, 1985) —managing conflict or leading people through conflict to resolution.

This book is designed for leaders to deal with the communication issues they confront. The concepts come from a variety of fields—communication, organizational theory, and practice—and are blended with suggestions for leaders.

The underlying notion is that if those who are charged with moving an organization forward can communicate effectively, it will be easier to implement programs successfully and the attendant problems will be fewer and less intense. Effective communication is understanding how people prefer to communicate and interact, what motivates them, and what happens when their needs go unmet.

While focusing on the *how*, I do not mean to discount the importance of the *what*. The content of messages is the meat of moving an organization forward.

The ideas and objectives that germinate the direction and plans for organizational success are critical. The way in which we transmit those points into action is the *process* of communicating to connect with others.

One area of discussion is a look at chaos, one of the things seldom under our control in life. We try to plan for it through budgeting—our time and our resources—but things happen personally and professionally over which we have little or no control. Dealing with unplanned events is chaotic. Attempting to control these events and the actions of others can be trying and enervating . . . and highly intrusive.

For your consideration, I present:

1. some ideas based on research,
2. a look at different types of people,
3. suggestions for dealing with examples of situations you may encounter,
4. techniques for judging the effectiveness of new skills, and
5. suggestions for keeping yourself and those with whom you interact energized.

As with my previous writings, I agonized over how to write this book. The first part has a decidedly didactic tone, imparting information and ideas with the appropriate support from the field. As I got into more of the Process Communication concepts, my writing relaxed a bit.

For those of you who prefer a more casual style, I hope you will forgive the more formal writing. For those of you who prefer the structure of a more academic style, I hope you will savor the relaxed passages.

For all of you, I trust you will enjoy what you read, find value and good ideas in what is presented, be able to reflect on past and future practice, see ways to connect with your coworkers and the significant other people in your life, and set a course for yourself.

Your ability to be an effective leader comes from who you are, how well you can get your own needs met and keep yourself motivated, and your powers of effective listening and observation to assist others. On your journey, you will meet people who may stimulate you—first by asking you to understand how people behave (and miscommunicate), and then by challenging you to recognize whose problem it is and finding the right person and technique to address it.

You will be introduced to six people. Each represents a different Personality Type. The character strengths, interaction styles, perceptions, needs, and patterns of miscommunication described about them are universal (Kahler, 2010).

(Please note that the people you meet are presented as "pure" types. None of us is. We are a composite of all six types. Will you interpret that each personality is in us, in varying degrees?)

You face the aspects of personality every day in the world of organizational life (and beyond). If you refine these basic aspects of understanding people with care and learn to identify their subtleties with skill and attention, you will enhance your ability to lead and empower others.

Leadership *tools* vary with each "builder" and insofar as the interaction ingredients vary. *Effectiveness* emerges when we understand why people do what they do.

Do you know what motivates a person to be successful, to accomplish, and to achieve? And do you know what leads the same person into negative, nonproductive behavior? If your answer is yes, then you hold the key to being an effective leader by having the right tools.

This book is adapted from an eclectic but practical body of knowledge that will help you translate the observable behaviors of others into useful and effective patterns of interaction for each person in your work life. (You will find there is also a carryover to your personal life.)

I invite you to examine your leadership, communication, and interaction skills and styles as you discover how to solve the problems in your life. As I have used these concepts in my personal and professional life, I have experienced one of the most dramatic metamorphoses one can imagine.

Those with whom I interact and those who have asked me to mentor them have said this information is among the most important and enlightening for them as well. I trust you will find it equally valuable. Perhaps, when you finish reading this book, you, too, may say, "Ah ha!"

REFERENCES

Bennis, W., & Nanus, B. (1985). *Leaders: The strategies of taking charge.* New York: Harper & Row.

Gilbert, M. B. (2012). *Communicating effectively: Tools for educational leaders* (2nd ed.). Lanham, MD: Rowman & Littlefield Education.

Kahler, T. (2010). *The mastery of management.* Little Rock, AR: Kahler Communications, Inc.

Section I

RAW MATERIALS: LEADERSHIP CONCEPTS

Chapter One

The Beginning Stage

Leaders may be defined as goal-directed people who can influence others to follow a path toward that goal. Leaders encourage others to go to places they would not go by themselves (Barker, 1999).

Leaders may be titular—that is, vested with the authority to lead by virtue of their position in an organization—or they may be genuine—able to lead regardless of their organizational status. In effective organizations, titular leaders are also genuine leaders.

Historically, many administrators embrace an approach to leadership that is quite parental. They view the organization as a quasi-family, with all the major decisions made by the family head. This approach disables or disenfranchises the professionals within the organization from important decisions that affect them.

If professional staff are *controlled* because others make decisions for them, it is not unusual to see these staff members adopt a controlling attitude with others. In this type of organization, people are not led; they are pushed.

> Perhaps a bit of folklore: It has been said that during his tenure as commander of the Allied forces in World War II, General Dwight Eisenhower used the following analogy to exemplify leadership. He said that if a string is laid on the floor and pushed at one end, not much happens. However, if one pulls the string, a lot more progress is made. Leading can be seen as "pulling the string," encouraging others to go in new directions.

Distinguishing between pushing and pulling might compare to bossing and leading. *Bossing* is characterized as telling without asking for input, evaluating without collaborating, and coercing others to perform. *Leading* involves others by seeking their input, looking to them as primary sources of performance evaluation, and trusting coworkers to make appropriate decisions in a collegial way (Glasser, 1990).

These characteristics are similar to the archetypal Theory X and Theory Y propositions offered by Douglas McGregor (1960). Theory X presumes subordinates need to be controlled and will not work well without stringent oversight. Theory Y presumes subordinates will contribute to the goals of the organization because there is something intrinsically gratifying about doing a good job; these people need minimal oversight.

The common distinctions are being *parental* or being *collegial*. The former invites others to be child-like and subservient; the latter encourages staff to be active participants in organizational decision making.

COMMUNICATE TO SUCCEED

In many respects, effective leadership relates to your ability to communicate and your willingness to understand issues from another person's perspective. Many people have difficulties in their professional and personal lives because of poorly developed or poorly used communication skills.

Simply stated, communication is understanding what another wants to convey. Developing your communication skills is tied inexorably to being an effective leader.

Understanding what people need as individuals is a principal determinant in effective communication. This is embedded in the interaction among leaders, colleagues, and subordinates. There are significant relationships between personality traits of people and their behavior and performance. (See Appendix A for an examination of this issue.)

The impact of different personality characteristics and needs is important in work environments. It is important that leaders understand how people interact and how personality types can affect organizational effectiveness.

Their personality types affect . . .

- how well leaders analyze needs,
- how much time they spend on oversight and management,
- how much time employees engage in productive activity, and
- how well all move toward organizational goals.

It is crucial to match leading style with communication preferences (Gilbert, 1996; 1999; 2011). This principle may be mitigated by opportunity—that is, staff may not have a full range of styles because of their preferences or their ability to use other strategies.

Other roadblocks may be organizational structure or size. Some organizations are arranged into self-contained units, providing little interaction among professional staff in planning or projects.

Organizations may also be constrained by size. If there is only one worker overseeing a specific function, then the range of problem-solving possibilities is limited to that person's background and experience. The effectiveness of small organization managers may depend on their communication effectiveness or involving their work forces in problem solving.

The extension to how organizations and their staffs are administered is not a quantum leap. It is important that those who supervise activities have a full range of decision styles—*telling, selling, participating* (or consulting) and *delegating* (or joining) (Hersey, Blanchard, & Johnson, 2013). All are appropriate, and one should not be used exclusively.

Choosing a decision style is based on factors in the situation, the leader, and those who participate in various organizational decisions. In effective organizations, those who implement decisions should make them—decisions should be made as close to the point of implementation as possible.

Full use of this strategy depends on the time available to make a decision and the maturity of those who would make those decisions. The choice of effective decision styles is based on what people need.

The decision styles should relate, in part to the *communication styles* (discussed below) of *directing, requesting, nurturing,* and *emoting*. Again, none is used exclusively and depends on what is needed at the moment.

The determination of decision styles and the effective communication used to help people succeed are the focus of this book.

AUDIENCES TO CONSIDER

Leaders deal with a number of different audiences, inside and outside of the organization. Each of these audiences holds a different stake in what the organization is about and what it produces. Effective communicators must know how to deal with each audience in ways that satisfy their need to know and to function well.

The various audiences include staff, customers, vendors, and the larger community. Each group needs to know different things.

- Staff need to know the building blocks ("whats") and tools and strategies ("hows") of their jobs.
- Customers want to know how the products work and where to go for help.

- Vendors need to know delivery schedules, so they can produce materials in a timely fashion.
- Communities (society) want to know how well the outcomes of the organization's work fit into an overall plan for the future.

MOVING AHEAD

The deft shift in communication styles distinguishes a leader from a manager. Effective leaders adjust their styles to help others meet their needs.

The greatest benefit of more effective communication is that it spreads throughout the organization—among administrators and staff, staff and customers, and staff with each other. Moreover, this benefit carries over into the home, where communication becomes more effective between the participants and their families.

(One critical concept is that individuals must be psychically energized—i.e., motivated—to perform well. This means they must get their psychological and physical needs met regularly.)

Many managers subscribe to the notion that staff must be structured into specific patterns in order for them to succeed. This narrow view limits people and thwarts their success.

Understanding ourselves and others, knowing what negative behaviors mean and what to do about them in professional (and personal) settings, and focusing more on *how* we communicate may have profound consequences in our effectiveness as people.

EFFECTIVE LEADERSHIP

Leaders confront conflict of one type or another on a fairly regular basis. This conflict may be productive, or it may cause varying degrees of unrest and damage to working relationships.

Conflict may be personal (within oneself), behavioral (involving interaction), or structural (relationships between different aspects of an organization) (Bondesio, 1992). Conflict ususally involves two or more people with incompatible positions or perspectives. Perhaps it is better described as the *perception* of incompatible positions. (As some have said, "Perception is reality.")

The management—moreover, the resolution—of conflict is the ongoing test of administrative effectiveness. If one can communicate effectively, one can attempt to resolve most, if not all, conflicts with more tools to change perspectives or to use differing perspectives to arrive at a *mutually acceptable* resolution.

One may choose from among five strategies or techniques of conflict management (see Chapter 11 for a more extensive discussion). The possibilities range from *withdrawal* and *suppression* to *domination, compromise* and *integration* (or *collaboration*).

Whether one ignores conflict or takes a position where dissatisfaction remains, the conflict is likely to resurface. (If the conflict causes the relationship to disintegrate, then the conflict may no longer be an issue because the competing parties do not interact with each other.) The true resolution of conflict involves both parties being satisfied—the *win/win* position.

In order to get to that juncture, one must be adept in understanding the position of the other party to the conflict and also be able to assert an alternate position in a palatable manner. To do this requires productive communication. The target position would then be *"I'm OK—You're OK"* (Berne, 1964; Ernst, 1973; Harris, 1969; Harris & Harris, 1985).

From the classical, eclectic background literature of management and administration, one of the requisites of organization is that "there are persons able to communicate with each other" (Barnard, 1938, p. 82). Further, communication occupies "a central place, because the structure, extensiveness, and scope of organization are almost entirely determined by communication techniques" (p. 91).

Conversely, "the absence of a suitable technique of communication would eliminate the possibility of some purposes as a basis for organization" (p. 90). In sum, "the first executive function is to develop and maintain a system of communication" (p. 226).

When one applies communication psychologically to administrative decisions,

> General organization decisions can control the behavior of the individual only through psychological mechanisms that bring values and knowledge to bear upon each individual decision at the time it is made. . . . Failures in communication result whenever it is forgotten that the behavior of individuals is the tool with which the organization achieves its purpose. (Simon, 1957, pp. 107–8)

Channels of communication are not necessarily tied to lines of authority. Functional communication is broad within an organization.

Personal motivation becomes part of the "formula" in organizational communication, especially when the communication may be informal. Moreover, effective messaging is affected by the degree to which it is received accurately.

The role of the receiver in organizational communication is a key. Messages are not *communicated* unless there is understanding of what those who send messages intend. This adds a dimension that some writers and practitioners of management and administration ignore—the *effective* individual relies on the degree of understanding and does not presume that the position of authority is enough to cause communication to occur.

One should not infer that titular authority is sufficient for communication. The willingness of subordinates and colleagues to receive (and understand) messages is crucial.

People come into organizations as *independent* (free-standing and autonomous). As they become acculturated to and active within organizations, they become *interdependent* (linked with, and possibly reliant upon, others).

The effective person should seek first to understand, then be understood (Covey, 1989). This wise advice leads to a discussion of empathic communication—understanding the perceptions of others is as a key to connecting with them. "Few people have had any training in listening . . ." (p. 238).

Seeking to empathize first is converse to what individuals do typically. We seek first to be understood. Most people do not listen with the intent to understand; they listen with the intent to reply. They're either speaking or preparing to speak. They're filtering everything through their own paradigms, reading their autobiography into other people's lives (Covey, 1989, p. 239).

As we focus on our own filters and *needs* (see Chapter 3), we process information through one of four levels, different from empathy: *ignoring* (not really listening), *pretending*, *selective listening* (focusing only on parts of the conversation), or *attentive listening* (paying attention to the words that are being spoken and the nuances that accompany them). The highest form of listening is *empathic,* getting inside another person's frame of reference to understand that person's perspective (Covey, 1989, p. 240).

Once you have understood one another, then you can move into your own frame and "seek to be understood." The power of empathy provides an entrée and invitation for others to connect with you. (More will be said about this when we look at techniques of understanding, including reflection.)

"Effective leaders employ several principles of effective communication. One of the most important is the awareness that different individuals respond to different communication styles" (Morford & Willing, 1993, p. 9).

The negative outcome of failing to acknowledge and practice this precept is that "perceived lack of interpersonal sensitivity is a major factor in derailing leaders' careers" (p. 9). Two other key principles are emphasized—the important link between trust and communication, leading to consistency, and understanding what the other person is really saying (supported by Covey's position).

Administrators confront crises (perhaps one step up from conflicts). These crises may be *personal* or related to *other individuals, groups, communication, finances,* or *major disasters*. Whether one confronts crises or conflicts, their effectiveness is measured by the degree to which all parties are satisfied with the eventual decisions and outcomes—win/win, or I'm OK/You're OK. Some common-sense guidelines for success in practical administration:

1. ownership of the problem to be addressed (see "Whose monkey is it?" in the Prologue to this book);
2. the value of selective neglect;
3. the importance of empowerment, enthusiasm, and effective communication; and
4. the need for positive reinforcement, cultivation of support, and good relations with primary and secondary stakeholders. (Salmon in Shannon, 1994)

Organizations are organic, dynamic, and subject to the pressures and requirements of a changing society. One of the evolutionary aspects of administration is a movement away from traditional "parental" oversight to shared leadership and participatory decision making.

In some cases, this evolution is glacial, slow-moving; in others, it is facilitated because of enthusiasm. To empower and encourage this change, effective administrators are visible, communicate honestly, accept others, are open and genuine, face problems confidently, and seek appropriate solutions (Kerry & Murdoch, 1993).

Conversely, "defective" organizations are described, in part, by

- perquisites for the very few,
- faulty communication,
- interest-group indulgence,
- poor professional relationships,
- literal interpretation of technicalities,
- imperial leadership,
- incoherent evaluation procedures,
- loss of control, and
- low stakeholder involvement (Gilman, 1992).

Failure to acknowledge the need for change and perseverance to hold too strongly to tradition, however outmoded, can doom organizations and their administrators.

"If what you're doing isn't working, stop! Find something that does work." We have been involved in organizational "insanity" for many years—continuing to perpetuate tradition without change in outcomes. If the outcomes are not salutary, we should scrap the strategies, plans, or policies, and adopt methods proven to produce effective outcomes.

Some time ago I attended a talk by a senior state executive who had moved from what some saw as a desirable location to one that was supposedly less desirable. Asked to explain his decision, he replied,

"Where I used to be, it took 11 people to change a light bulb—one person to change the bulb and ten to share the experience.

"Here, I found the number did not change. However, it was now one to change the bulb and ten to tell you how good the old bulb was."

We continue to worship a dim or dysfunctional bulb that no longer lights our way. Why? Because it is what we have always done, what we know.

We are reluctant to change, even in the face of prevailing evidence. Our fate is inextricably tied to finding new ways to be successful or living with outcomes that may eventually doom us.

Field-based research has demonstrated increasing emphasis on necessary skills for new administrators. Conceptual self-awareness and people skills are viewed as eminently more important than technical skills (McGrevin & Schmieder, 1993).

Communication, especially listening, is critical among the skills required for all administrators. Communication styles are one of the major areas of concern in administrator preparation (Pitner, 1989). Administrator preparation programs should include opportunities for individuals to develop skills to communicate accurately and effectively by utilizing appropriate listening (Pohland et al., 1988, p. 58).

"Careful analytical listening" (Peper, 1989, p. 363) is the *first minimum skill* for the clinical education of leaders. Skill in communication is the *most important competency* in terms of individual effectiveness and success (Gousha & Mannan, 1991).

The relationship between effective listening and satisfaction with supervision has been demonstrated. If staff perceive their supervisors to listen effectively, it predicts the degree to which they are satisfied with job supervision (Tackett, 2000).

Again, perception is the key. A positive perspective of one aspect generates a positive view of another. As conflict may be the *perception* of incompatible goals, so, too, is perception a strong factor in determining job satisfaction. (The preference for interacting with those who are similar is confirmed in other research [Knaupp, n. d.].)

STANDARDS

Emphasis for effective communication is found in the various stated and implied standards for administration. While these standards do not focus singly on communication, the outcomes of effective communication are embedded within the standards and their indicators.

Specific to the context of this book are *performance indicators* relating to communication. *The leader demonstrates skills required to* . . .

- work collaboratively with staff.
- model distributed leadership skills and involve staff in decision-making processes.
- use collaboration strategies to collect, analyze, and interpret organizational information and to communicate information about the organization to the community at-large.
- develop appropriate communication skills to advocate for democracy, equity, and diversity.

The emphasis appears obvious: It is crucial that leaders understand the messages that the various stakeholders in the enterprise want these leaders to understand and in the way they want the messages understood. As a result, both pre-service and in-service professional development of leaders should include direct and integrated preparation in specific and applied communication skills.

These standards are broad-based and relate to leadership in general ways. Some prefer to look at administrative qualifications as they compare to former, tradition-based gender roles, where men are the hunter-gatherers and women are the child-bearing nurturers.

GENDER MYTHS AND REALITIES

Certain issues relate specifically to women in administration—networks and relationships and patterns of communication (Restine, 1993). The issue of gender is interesting because of traditional role models and perceived patterns of behavior and interaction. It is easy—maybe too easy—to presume that because women are traditionally *nurturers*, all women prefer or demonstrate nurturing behavior before all others (Stewart et al., 1990; Tannen, 1990).

Some may presume that women tend to effect a facilitative administrative style. Also, a similar presumption may be asserted about men. Since men have assumed most leadership roles traditionally, *all* men are born leaders and capable of demonstrating leadership traits as a function of gender.

Men may have been viewed traditionally as being administratively authoritative. (I offer that this perspective limits possibilities that may be available to effective leaders, regardless of their gender. These assertions may suggest patterns in need of further examination [see Chapter 4, Communication Blueprints].)

The reality is that preferred communication patterns relate more to who people are personally rather than attributable to their gender. Some women prefer the *report* orientation attributed to men; some men seek *rapport,* a trait often ascribed to women (Tannen, 1990).

The needs we have guide us more than the gender stereotypes we have seen. In fact, these stereotypes may mislead us if we use them in a way that denies what we need. Confusion can arise: "Men don't cry," or "Nice girls don't do *that.*"

A VISION FOR THE FUTURE

Some of the impetus attached to the changing role of leaders comes from initiatives in reform—organizational restructuring, role conflict, and changes in communication. When implemented, reforms suggest that administrators will facilitate increasingly shared governance, participant empowerment, and participatory decision making (Richardson et al. 1991). To be effective, these restructured functions have communication at their core.

While many reform efforts have focused on restructuring the participation of middle-level administrators, new or retooled patterns have been suggested for those at the top as well. Open communication is reported to be the key to success (Chance et al. 1991).

POINTS TO PONDER

- Communication is a requisite skill for effective leaders.
- More can be gained by leading rather than bossing.
- Traditional gender roles need to be re-examined.
- Communication occurs when understanding is present.

REFERENCES

Barker, J. L. (1999). *Leadershift: Five lessons for leaders in the 21st century.* St. Paul, MN: Star Thrower Productions (video).

Barnard, C. I. (1938). *The functions of the executive.* Cambridge, MA: Harvard University Press.

Berne, E. (1964). *Games people play: The psychology of human relationships.* New York, NY: Grove Press.

Bondesio, M. J. (1992, August). *Conflict management at school: An unavoidable task.* Paper presented at the regional conference of the Commonwealth Council for Educational Administration, Hong Kong. (ERIC Document Reproduction Service No. ED355655)

Chance, E. W. et al. (1991, October). *Long-term rural superintendents: Characteristics and attributes.* Paper presented at the annual convention of the National Rural Education Association, Jackson, MS. (ERIC Document Reproduction Service No. ED339572)

Covey, S. R. (1989). *The 7 habits of highly effective people: Powerful lessons in personal change.* New York, NY: Simon & Schuster.

Ernst, F. (1973). Psychological rackets in the OK corral. *Transactional Analysis Journal, 3*(2), 19–23.

Gilbert, M. B. (1996). The Process Communication Model: Understanding ourselves and others. *NASSP Bulletin, 80*(578), 75–80.

Gilbert, M. B. (1999). Why educators have problems with some students: Understanding frames of preference. *Journal of Educational Administration, 37*, 243–55. (ERIC Document Accession No. EJ592943)

Gilbert, M. B. (2011, July). *Connecting with students for academic success: An examination of the Process Education Model.* Paper presented at the 6th Education for a Changing Environment Conference, Manchester, England.

Gilman, D. A. (1992). This issue: Correlates of a defective school. *Contemporary Education, 63*(2), 89–90. (ERIC Document Reproduction Service No. EJ447974)

Glasser, W. (1990). *The quality school: Managing students without coercion.* New York, NY: Harper & Row.

Gousha, R. P., & Mannan, G. (1991, August). *Analysis of selected competencies: Components, acquisition and measurement perceptions of three groups of stakeholders in education.* Paper presented at the annual meeting of the National Council of Professors of Educational Administration, Fargo, ND. (ERIC Document Reproduction Service No. ED336850)

Harris, A. B., & Harris, T. A. (1985). *Staying OK.* New York, NY: Harper & Row.

Harris, T. A. (1969). *I'm OK—You're OK: A practical guide to transactional analysis.* New York, NY: Harper & Row.

Hersey, P., Blanchard, K., & Johnson, D. E. (2013). *Management of organizational behavior: Utilizing human resources* (10th ed.). Upper Saddle River, NJ: Pearson.

Kerry, T., & Murdoch, A. (1993). Education managers as leaders: Some thoughts on the context of the changing nature of schools. *School Organisation, 13,* 221–30. (ERIC Document Reproduction Service No. EJ472566)

Knaupp, J. (n.d.) *Preservice teachers' ranking of personality characteristics preferred by primary students, middle school students, parents and administrators.* Unpublished paper, Arizona State University.

McGregor, D. (1960). *The human side of enterprise.* New York, NY: McGraw-Hill.

McGrevin, C. E., & Schmieder, J. H. (1993, April). *Keys to success: Critical skills for the novice principal.* Paper presented at the annual meeting of the American Educational Research Association, Atlanta, Georgia. (ERIC Document Reproduction Service No. ED361852)

Morford, J. A., & Willing, D. (1993, March/April). Communication: Key to effective administration. *Adult Learning,* pp. 9–10.

Peper, J. B. (1989). Clinical education for school superintendents and principals: The missing link. In D. E. Griffiths, R. T. Stout & P. B. Forsyth (Eds.), *Leaders for America's schools: The reports and papers of the national commission on excellence in educational administration* (pp. 360–66). Berkeley, CA: McCutchan.

Pitner, N. J. (1989). School administrator preparation: The state of the art. In D. E. Griffiths, R. T. Stout & P. B. Forsyth (Eds.), *Leaders for America's schools: The reports and papers of the national commission on excellence in educational administration* (pp. 367–402). Berkeley, CA: McCutchan.

Pohland, P., Milstein, M., Schilling, N., & Tonigan, J. S. (1988). Emergent issues in the curriculum of educational administration. In F. C. Wendel & M. T. Bryant (Eds.), *New directions for administrator preparation* (pp. 37–61). Tempe, AZ: University Council for Educational Administration.

Restine, L. N. (1993). *Women in administration: Facilitators for change.* Newbury Park, CA: Corwin Press. (ERIC Document Reproduction Service No. ED358565)

Richardson, M. D., et al. (1991, November). *The changing role of the school principal: A research synthesis.* Paper presented at the annual meeting of the Mid-South Educational Research Association, Louisville, KY. (ERIC Document Reproduction Service No. ED345320)

Shannon, T. A. (1994, April). Salmon's laws. *Executive Educator,* 52–54. (ERIC Document Reproduction Service No. EJ481340)

Simon, H. A. (1965). *Administrative behavior: A study of decision-making processes in administrative organization* (2nd ed.). New York, NY: The Free Press.

Stewart, L. P., Stewart, A. D., Friedley, S. A., & Cooper, P. J. (1990). *Communication between the sexes: Sex differences and sex-role stereotypes.* Scottsdale, AZ: Gorsuch Scarisbrick.

Tackett, J. D. (2000). *Self-reported teacher job satisfaction and perceptions of administrative listening skills.* Unpublished doctoral dissertation, University of Arkansas at Little Rock.

Tannen, D. (1990). *You just don't understand: Men and women in conversation.* New York, NY: William Morrow.

Chapter Two

Chaos

The Wrinkling of Order and Logic

As a leader, you can anticipate that planning will go awry, that things will occur over which you have no control, and that your life will not be as orderly as you had hoped. Many administrators try to order their lives and the life of their organization by controlling the environment and the people in it.

This is *parental* administration. It may seem to work, but in the end, it is not long-lasting. At some point, things will come crashing down, much to the dismay of the person who thought he or she "had it under control."

Two fallacies get in the way of parental administration: (1) attempting to subjugate the staff has no negative results, and (2) if I maintain control, nothing can go wrong. The first myth is based on the delusion that you have the ability to control others. Not so. People may seem to comply, but the question arises whether they are complying willingly and enthusiastically, or just going through the motions. I suggest the latter.

The second myth either stems from or leads to administrative arrogance. "I have the title; therefore, I must be in control." Titular authority is not necessarily virtual authority—those who would be led verify an administrator's right to act by complying with directives.

PARENTAL ADMINISTRATION

I observed a school district fraught with tension and conflict for ten years. The board was almost always divided on issues and were constantly looking for the right change agent. They failed.

They hired five superintendents over the ten years, each of whom had a four-year contract. Doing the quick calculation, you realize that no one ever completed a term. The costs to the district were great—in terms of time, lack of progress, and buy-out dollars.

The reality was that the district staff would listen to the *change du jour*, then continue what they had been doing, waiting for the next regime to be installed. This is a logical consequence (Dreikurs & Grey, 1993) of constant change.

People resist change with their every fiber. Organizations in a state of constant flux will not progress much because the staff want, prefer, and need some times of stasis.

The more long-lasting approach is *collegial leadership*. To say it simply: decisions should be made as close to the point of implementation as possible. Ownership of decisions raises the level of involvement—and accountability for the results of the decisions.

It is less time-consuming to be a parental administrator. You make the decision and direct others to implement it. You also presume that because *you* made the decision, it will be implemented. Here, you need to apply the litmus test of leadership—turn around and see if anyone is following. If there is no one there, you are just going for a stroll.

This consequence follows Barnard's (1938) timeless counsel: to be a functional executive, do not issue orders that encourage staff to be non-compliant. Titular authority (the right to act) does not verify actual authority. If your staff do not do what they are told (whether insubordinate or not), your effectiveness is challenged.

> As a young and fresh administrator, I told the staff that we were embarking on a new program (endorsed by the organization). I was enthusiastic and had just returned from intensive training on the new program.
>
> The staff listened politely as I prescribed what we would be doing. I was satisfied and excited about their response (silence), which I interpreted as willingness to comply.
>
> As I walked the halls over the next weeks, I saw no difference. I was confused and puzzled. After all, I had made a decision, but nothing had changed.
>
> I brought the staff together and admitted that perhaps I had moved too quickly. I was still eager to see change that was promising, but I could not do it myself. We agreed that we would take the time they needed to be informed better. It worked.

The point is that any administrator must be collegial and involve the staff in decisions that are rightly theirs to make. *Their followership verifies your leadership.*

CHAOS

The effective leader must have facility in dealing with five major organizational components—authority, communication, productivity, morale, and change (Caplow, 1983). Stated so simply, this notion seems irreverent.

In a perfect world, where managers have control of inputs, outputs, and the environment, it is possible to *run* an organization with this orderly template. But the world is not orderly, nor are the people in it perfect.

Organizational theory, like any scientific explanation, attempts to predict patterns (of behavior, in this instance) from consistent synthesis of components or concepts. Planning for the future is based on reviewing the past and accounting for some change in the environment.

We look to statistics and probability to anchor our decisions. It is all very scientific, isn't it?

Yes, it is, if the variables do not change much. However, where classic science stops, *chaos* begins (Gleick, 1987).

While science is "an orderly process of asking questions and finding their answers" (Kuhn in Gleick, 1987, p. 36), chaos "can be characterized as the study of orderly disorder created by simple processes" (p. 266). The disorder comes from an inability to control the environment and the forces that can affect an organization.

It is scary; it is discomfiting. We like order.

Chaos shakes the foundation(s) of established practice. It creates turbulence that upsets the *status quo.* This turbulence can be so slight as to be imperceptible—the butterfly effect, the sensitive dependence on initial conditions (Feynman in Gleick, 1987). The slightest change in leadership style or behavior can have a far-reaching impact (Daljit, 2009). However, a constant state of flux is inimical to organizational functioning.

As upsetting as it can be, chaos can stimulate a creativity to organize new patterns of behaviors and operations—sometimes stable, sometimes unstable—to set a new path. If effective leaders recognize the need to deal with changing elements, they can either instigate or coalesce these new patterns.

Chaos stimulates organizational autonomy from its environment and the development of "new capacities to make it [the organization] increasingly resourceful" (Wheatley, 2006, p. 84). In the burgeoning global economy and interdependence, organizations and their leaders must be responsive to the "turbulence" that pervades the world.

Organizational evolution must be driven by a conscious intelligence to deal with current change and scan the environment for elements that will presage future change. The suggested foresight is to eliminate, as much as possible, the "fantasy of deterministic probability" (Gleick, 1987, p. 6).

RE-ESTABLISHING STABILITY

The moving pendulum of issues foments serious dissatisfaction with the *status quo*. The arrogance of many institutions as seemingly the "only game in town" is challenged by demands for change.

Changes germinate from dissatisfaction with traditional ways of providing services and products. Alternatives have challenged tradition—organizational websites, electronic sales, disappearing locations. Witness the number of brick-and-mortar retail outlets that have succumbed to etail and online ordering.

Debates that seem to many to be benign and well intentioned reveal depths of animosity and suspicion when exposed to light (Glass, 2008, pp. 200-201). How to deal with performance and effectiveness may relate more to the differences in a changing environment and global economy than to organizational structure.

Most leaders are predominantly three (out of six possibilities [see Chapter 4]) types of people—those who are compassionate and want to help others, those who think the key to success is developing clear thought patterns and logic, and those who believe that the truth, important concepts, and values are prerequisites to success.

With regard to administrators, different resources are used to achieve desired goals through interaction according to their beliefs and values (the third type of leader mentioned above). A fourth type, action-orientation, may thrive long-term but only with sufficient energy, either from within or having staff with the necessary strengths to help with success.

Those who have ascended the administrative ladder hold clear values, preferred influence over power, and utilized effective interpersonal and communication skills (Hall, 1994). Wise administrators establish and maintain good communication with their staff, leading to trust and more effective administration (Lewis, 1994).

Effective leaders focus on transactional communication, different sources of influence, and respect for the individual, all of which underpin a "blueprint" of the effort needed from each group of stakeholders in the venture (Schmuck & Schmuck, 1992). When carrying this to the highest level of governance—the policy making and planning that occurs between the board and the administration—effective communication is the key to that relationship. When this is translated into team building, employees are enabled to communicate in a way that facilitates effective team functioning (Southard, 1993).

The implications are clear—effective communication is a requisite, if not the most important, skill area for effective leadership. The skills involved in effective communication should be part of the pre-service preparation and part of the continuing professional development of administrators.

What is missing is a clear direction for this preparation. The next chapters will discuss specifics of effective communication (beginning with developing effective listening skills), explicate a model—Process Communication (Kahler, 1995)—that will allow leaders to achieve the goal of successful communication, and examine possibilities for leaders to refine their communication skills. Each of us is different and prefers different ways of experiencing the world—that is, to be effective different builders use different tools.

Using chaos to the advantage of the organization is the pre-eminent challenge for leaders. The following guidance may assist policy makers and policy administrators:

- Establish and identify your non-negotiables;
- Maintain stability but embrace change;
- Plan for the best but prepare for the worst;
- Attend to the small things for the biggest effect;
- Be cautiously bold when implementing change;
- Judiciously welcome feedback, but not too much nor too little; and
- Treat problems as solutions waiting to happen. (Shoup & Studer, 2010, p. 123)

Reaping order out of chaos bodes well for the leader and the organization. It does not guarantee smooth sailing and no conflict, but it is a start in the right and productive direction.

POINTS TO PONDER

- Decisions should be made as close to the point of implementation as practical.
- Followership verifies leadership.
- Effective communication is a requisite of effective leadership.

REFERENCES

Barnard, C. I. (1938). *The functions of the executive.* Cambridge, MA: Harvard University Press.

Caplow, T. (1983). *Managing an organization* (2nd ed.). New York, NY: Holt, Rinehart & Winston.

Daljit, N. (2009). *A chaotic view of leadership: Applying chaos theory to the enactment of presidential leadership.* Unpublished doctoral dissertation, Central Michigan University.

Dreikurs, R., & Grey, L. (1993). *Logical consequences.* New York, NY: Plume Books.

Glass, G. V. (2008). *Fertilizers, pills, and magnetic strips: The fate of public education in America.* Charlotte, NC: Information Age Publishing.

Gleick, J. (1987) *Chaos: Making a new science.* New York, NY: Penguin Books.

Hall, V. (1994). *Making a difference: Women headteachers' contribution to schools as learning institutions.* Paper presented at the annual meeting of the British Educational Management and Administration Society, Manchester, England. (ERIC Document Reproduction Service No. ED376579)

Kahler, T. (1995). *The Process Communication Model seminars.* Little Rock, AR: Kahler Communications, Inc.

Lewis, P. M. (1994, February). Communication techniques: Building better relationships with academic personnel. *Business Officer,* 38–40. (ERIC Document Reproduction Service No. EJ477919)

Schmuck, R. A., & Schmuck, P. A. (1992). *Small districts, big problems: Making school everybody's house.* Newbury Park, CA: Corwin Press. (ERIC Document Reproduction Service No. ED370747)

Shoup, J. R., & Studer, S. C. (2010). *Leveraging chaos: The mysteries of leadership and policy revealed.* Lanham, MD: Rowman & Littlefield.

Southard, S. (1993, March/April). *Total quality management (Team building and cross training): From business to academe and back again to business.* Paper presented at the annual meeting of the Conference on College Composition and Communication, San Diego, CA. (ERIC Document Reproduction Service No. ED359567)

Wheatley, M. (2006). *Leadership and the new science: Discovering order in a chaotic world.* San Francisco, CA: Berrett-Koehler.

Chapter Three

The Start of Communication

LISTENING

Saying it right begins with understanding the message *before* responding. This echoes Covey's "Seek first to understand."

The key to effective interaction is interpreting what others want us to understand. As humans interacting with others, we communicate a substantial majority of each day. This means that most of our waking hours are spent *writing, reading, speaking,* or *listening*. In today's world, that includes texting and other forms of electronic communication.

Prior to the advent of electronic communication and in a time when face-to-face interaction was more prevalent, pioneers in the field of listening—Paul Rankin (1928), Ralph Nichols (1956), Lyman Steil (1984, 1991), and others—have said that listening is a skill taught inversely to its use. More specifically, the average person spends a part of each day in listening situations, while receiving little or no formal training in listening. Moreover, we are (still) taught various components and nuances of writing all the way through formal schooling; yet, this is a skill used eventually about 10% or less of the time.

So when do we learn how to listen? Many times the only listening training we receive is the check for attention: "Did you hear what I said?" Or the reminder that we are not listening: "I don't think you understand."

But what is listening? It "is the process of attending to, making meaning from and responding to spoken and/or nonverbal messages" (International Listening Association, 1996, p. 2).

Before we get into the more formal listening situations—such as in school or on the job—we may see ineffective listening by parents and other adults. When individuals encounter ineffective listening early in life and base their

Table 3.1. Communication Skills Learning

Skill	When Learned
Writing	Pre-Kindergarten-Graduate
Reading	Pre-Kindergarten-Grade 8
Speaking	First six months of life
Listening	?

own listening on the patterns they experience, it is very difficult to change those patterns later. First impressions abide.

Humans listen before they speak, speak before they read, and read before they write. Thus, failure to refine our listening skills impairs the entire process of human communication (Wolff et al. 1983, p. 24).

Additionally, a large percentage of people are extrinsic in their interaction preferences (to be discussed below). Listening is internal.

Some measures of listening are *summarizing, drawing inferences, recalling facts accurately,* and *recalling facts in sequence* (Barker, 1971). The point here is that listening is undertaught, and the consequences of poor listening are compounded within one's life.

Effective leaders should be sure that their listening skills are adequate to address the many times their attention is sought during the work day. Also, appropriate emphasis should be given to reinforcing careful listening throughout the organization.

To start on a small and independent scale, leaders might make a commitment to change their own listening habits (and encourage others to follow their lead). Here are some suggestions for improvement (Lyle, 1984):

1. Realize that listening takes real effort: *Be prepared to expend time and energy.*
2. Look at the person who is speaking to you: *Do not fake attention or seem uninterested.*
3. Turn off feelings as much as possible and listen with an open mind: *Receive information as fresh; suppress your bias.*
4. Do not jump to conclusions; hear the person out: *Do not interrupt.*
5. *Separate fact from inference.*
6. Listen between the lines to hear what is not being said: *Are you getting all the information?*
7. Learn to read nonverbal communication: *What are the person's posture and movements telling you?*
8. Pay attention to the feedback you provide: *Have you confirmed, corrected, or clarified your understanding of the message?*

There are few who would question the importance of effective communication. The key to change is for those in positions of decision making to recognize the need and to address that need.

The information presented here may raise the questions to be answered and may provide the basis for change for those who wish to do so. These ideas also underpin how we can become effective leaders.

Caveat: While listening is important for those who communicate in the auditory mode, one should recognize that other skills and preferences should be considered. Multi-modal delivery, especially with all of the technology available today, should become part of a leader's repertoire.

LISTENING TO COMMUNICATE

Communicating is conveying a message that is understood by others in the way you intend. Messages pass through various screens as they are received. These screens may muddle messages and their understanding. Prior experiences, feelings, beliefs, physical state, and conflicting agenda all may serve to lead one in a direction different from what the sender intends. Figure 3.1 shows the communication process (adapted from Steil, 1984).

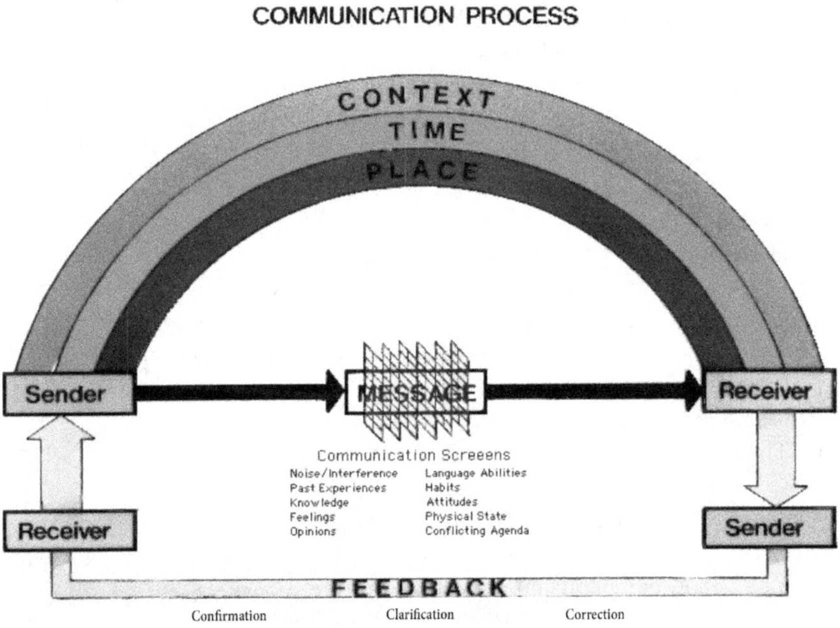

COMMUNICATION PROCESS

CONTEXT
TIME
PLACE

Sender → MESSAGE → Receiver

Communication Screens
Noise/Interference   Language Abilities
Past Experiences   Habits
Knowledge   Attitudes
Feelings   Physical State
Opinions   Conflicting Agenda

Receiver ← **FEEDBACK** ← Sender
Confirmation   Clarification   Correction

Figure 3.1. Communication Rainbow

To check for understanding, the message is looped from sender to receiver and back again. Additionally, one has a better chance of communicating if the time, place, and context are appropriate.

If it is the wrong time or place or situation, the process may be confounded. Trying to tell a colleague of an important meeting when she has just come from the doctor's office with heavy news is not likely to be successful, even though the message may be simple.

In this day of asynchronous communication (texting, email, etc.), clarifying understanding may be postponed. Also, communicating from different locations may compound the difficulty of comprehending messages.

The Key

The most critical communication skill, *listening*, is the one that is taught the least. In fact, most people receive little or no formal training in the techniques of listening.

Adults (especially, leaders) are asked to listen a substantial part of their day in organizational settings (Rankin, 1928); yet, the average listener can recall only 50% of a message immediately after it has been delivered. This rate drops to 25% in a very short period. Therefore, the average person may be *75% ineffective* as a listener (Steil, Barker & Watson, 1983). If asked, most people would support the idea of listening as an important skill, but becoming a proficient listener may be something for *others* to do, much like observing the speed limits on the highways.

Many hold some *misconceptions* about listening:

1. Listening is a matter of intelligence.
2. Good hearing and good listening are closely associated.
3. Listening is an automatic reflex.
4. Daily practice eliminates the need for training in listening.
5. Learning to read will automatically improve listening.
6. Learning to read is more important than learning to listen.
7. The speaker is totally responsible for success in oral communication.
8. Listening is essentially passive.
9. Listening means agreement.
10. The consequences of careless listening are minimal. (Wolff et al. 1983)

What is actual is what occurs when "not" is added to each of the above statements. Because many do not understand fully what listening is and what listening is not, bad habits continue.

People who receive listening training perform at significantly higher levels than those who do not (Papa & Glenn, 1973). The implications are clear—*those who listen better, do better* (especially in an auditory environment).

How Administrators Listen

Administrators believe they are moderately good listeners. They see themselves as attentive and understanding, but note they may be distracted when their interest wanes, may presume to understand without checking back, or allow feelings about a speaker to interfere (Gilbert, 1984).

In the research study, administrators saw themselves proficient in understanding messages, being able to stay focused, and being able to sort through details for the overall message. Conversely, they indicated they had problems with attending when their interest waned, when they were distracted by the delivery or appearance of the speaker, and that they tended to try to understand a message (too?) quickly.

Table 3.2. Administrators' Listening Behaviors Perceptions

Most Proficient

1. I **rarely** don't understand so I quit listening.
2. It is **rarely** hard for me to keep up with a message because I can't figure out what might come next and I lose interest.
3. I **rarely** get so concerned with details that I have difficulty separating the key ideas from those that are only supporting.
4. I **rarely** find myself distracted easily, so I miss part of the message and cannot figure out what is going on.

Least Proficient

1. I **sometimes** don't pay attention when I'm not interested in the subject.
2. My response to an oral message is **frequently** based on my initial understanding of that message.
3. I **sometimes** judge speakers mainly on delivery style and appearance.

(Note: With respect to item 2 under "Least Proficient," responses based on initial understanding may be faulty if one does not check for accuracy.)

To reiterate: *Communication* occurs when the listener understands a message in the same way the speaker intended that it be understood. Failure to employ feedback—to confirm, clarify, or correct a message—can lead to misunderstanding.

Barriers to listening effectiveness—*being distracted, being ready to listen, anticipation, interrupting, planning for a response,* and *thinking of other things*—can get in the way of interacting successfully (Gilbert, 1989).

There is consensus on two areas of proficiency and deficiency. Table 3.3 shows the agreement (Gilbert, 1989).

Table 3.3. Staff Perceptions of Administrators' Listening

Most Proficient

1. Rarely don't understand so quit listening.
2. Rarely hard to keep up with a message because can't figure out what might come next and lose interest.

Least Proficient

1. Sometimes get wrapped up in own argument and planning for a response.
2. Response sometimes based on initial understanding.

Staff members may assess their supervisor's overall performance as a supervisor in looking at the listening behaviors—that is, there may be a performance "halo." If the overall performance is perceived as being good, any subset of that performance, such as listening, is seen in the same light.

Also, staff might agree that their supervisors listen well if they grant requests—"If you give me what I want, then I know you have listened carefully. Conversely, if you do not give me what I ask for, then you obviously do not understand my request." Of course, understanding and compliance are not always closely linked.

> I remember an interaction I had with one of my daughters. She had asked me for something; I denied her request. She asked again—still no positive response from me. She then pouted, "You just don't understand!"
>
> Of course, this was a challenge to someone who had done substantial work in communication. I responded by clarifying my understanding of what she wanted.
>
> "Is that right?" I asked.
>
> "Yes," she said, surprised.
>
> "Then it's not that I don't understand. It's just that I am not giving you what you want."
>
> She turned and huffed away.

The point here is that *understanding* does not mean agreement, and lack of agreement may be construed as poor listening or ineffective communicating.

How administrators listen can have a notable impact on their staffs. That is, those who are perceived to listen well relate more positively to their staffs.

How to Listen Better

While the need to be an effective listener may be apparent, what might be done to improve? Since listening is a skill, one might consider these steps for improving skills:

- Understand the *need* for the skill.
- *Learn* the component steps.
- *Practice* the steps.
- Receive *feedback* on how well the skill is being performed.
- *Incorporate* the skill and its components into your repertoire.

The need for developing listening skills is critical for success. Leaders are but one group who might benefit from improving their listening. To put the meat on the bones of this learning skeleton, here are some suggestions:

KEYS TO EFFECTIVE LISTENING

1. *Find areas of interest*: Look for benefits and opportunities; ask "What's in this for me?"
2. *Judge content, not delivery*: Overlook delivery errors and concentrate on the main message.
3. *Hold your fire*: Withhold judgment until the message is complete. (This will be difficult if your belief system or authority is challenged.)
4. *Listen for ideas*: Focus on central themes.
5. *Be flexible*: Take appropriate notes, adapting to the speaker's style. (Of course, you should get into the habit of taking notes and not rely on memory. Your memory may not be as reliable as you desire.)
6. *Work at listening*: Exhibit active body readiness—eye contact, supportive facial expressions, etc. Ask clarifying questions and respond appropriately.
7. *Resist distractions*: Fight or avoid distractions; tolerate bad habits in others; know how to concentrate (and recognize when concentration is waning or absent).
8. *Exercise your mind*: Search for challenging material.
9. *Keep your mind open*: Know your emotional triggers and be prepared to combat their control over you.
10. *Capitalize on the fact that thought is faster than speech*: Challenge (mentally), anticipate, summarize, and reflect on what has been said; weigh

the evidence; listen between the lines. (Nichols & Stevens, 1956; Steil, Barker, & Watson, 1983)

Leading to More Effective Listening

With the hue and cry for excellence, administrators might want to address a persistent and vaguely recognized problem—people may not know how to listen because they have not been taught how. Telling them to "listen better" is not sufficient. Oral communication predominates in face-to-face communication. The leaders set the tone.

If the administrator is (or becomes) a proficient and effective listener, then others will see a model to be emulated. If staff recognize the value of listening well and can exhibit the skill, a major hurdle in the barrier to getting others to attend *mentally* will be overcome.

Do administrators listen well? They think that they do, but there are areas for improvement, especially in *barriers to effective listening*. The *Keys to Effective Listening* provide means for improving listening behaviors.

The roadblock is in understanding that a problem exists. The emphasis on listening as a crucial skill is not widespread; moreover, a potential problem might be masked by other interpersonal or organizational behavior deficiencies. Administrators who model and transmit good listening behaviors can go a long way to improving relationships and to becoming more effective leaders. (Cf. Steil & Bommelje, 2004.)

Reflective Listening

People want to talk more than they listen. In conversations, many think that controlling the interchange is the way to get one's point across and direct or persuade others.

Establishing rapport that leads to understanding may be a more productive way to proceed. I contend that this rapport is genderless, contrary to the assertion that rapport is a female trait (Tannen, 1990). While feeling-oriented people are decidedly female, they are not exclusively so. (See the description of *Harmonizers* in Chapter 4.)

The feedback loop depicted in the "Communication Rainbow" (in Figure 3.1) is a way to ensure that understanding has happened. Confirming, correcting, or clarifying a message are ways to verify the understanding. Another way to describe this aspect of communication is through *reflection*.

In reflective listening, we try to convey to the sender that we have understood—that she or he has communicated. We are looking for agreement of interpretation, not necessarily agreement of content. What we, as listeners, want is the sender to get to "Yes! That's it! You got it!" (cf. Fisher, Ury & Patton, 2011).

We paraphrase what we have heard in thought (and possibly feeling) until we get to "Yes!" (Bolton, 1979). If you get "yes . . . but," then understanding is not complete.

Part of the problem in turning ourselves outward to another perspective is that we have to *want* to understand and to *put aside* our own needs to accomplish that understanding. Some may think that "Yes!" means agreement.

If we have a different point of view or position, we may want to push our views or be unwilling to accept (not agree with) another idea or belief. To understand another means that we have to "listen" to the message from someone else's perspective.

To do this implies we have common "screens" (ways of filtering the message) and are willing to be empathic, or at least *shift*. (This notion of shifting will be expanded later.)

While *empathy* usually speaks to understanding how another feels, it may also describe looking at issues through another's eyes (screens), or walking the same path. The emphasis is staying receptive in order to understand. "Communication between persons . . . [is] a mysterious business that . . . is almost never achieved except in part" (Rogers, 1970, p. 11).

Understanding another empowers both you and the other person. You have opened yourself to build a relationship.

The other person has connected when she or he has been understood. There is a sense of satisfaction when communication occurs; however, we are not always successful.

Are You Listening to Me?

While we know there are measures to check if another *has listened,* we do not know at any moment if someone else *is listening*. We cannot get into someone's head to *see* if indeed they are attending to what we are saying or to something else.

Of course, we can observe attentive body language—eye contact, alert posture, etc.—to determine if our communication partner is prepared to listen, but we do not know if they *are* listening. We can ask questions to check for understanding.

We can determine if their responses are contextually accurate, but we do not *know* that listening is occurring. We can only determine if accurate listening has happened *after the fact*—when they have done what we have asked or directed, or if their responses reflect what we have wanted them to understand.

When the messages are not spoken or delivered at different times, our listening checks may be confounded. Newer technology has added greater opportunities for communicating and potential for greater "garbling."

Dealing with *Cyberspeak*

Listening is accomplished best when we are face-to-face, either with one person or a group of people. In this age of burgeoning technology, we can also hear and listen to others via telephone conversations and voice mail/messaging. What we give up on the phone is the "body language," or nonverbal cues that are most helpful when we look at someone.

In person, we might see their joy, instead of just listening to their excitement. We might note the tapping of a foot or pencil to indicate impatience, frustration, or nervousness.

Clear electronic transmission does not mean effective communication—that is, determining the receiver understood what was intended. It will be interesting to see how a proliferation of video connections (à la Skype, Zoom, Face Time, etc.) may add the nonverbal aspects to telephonic communication.

We further confound communication by making use of what might be called "cyberspeak"—email, chat, instant messaging, texting, and tweeting. We can talk to and with others synchronously (in a time-specific way, as in face-to-face conversation), or asynchronously (at different times, much in the way we respond to posted mail).

The problem with asynchronous messaging is that we lose any vocal qualities, in addition to the loss of visual cues. These losses increase the possibility of misunderstanding—hence, lack of communication, or the increased potential of miscommunication.

Sometimes our correspondents try to help using "cybercode." When someone wants to indicate smiling or being humorous, she or he may use "lol" (for "laughing out loud"), or visual (punctuation) code—emoticons or emojis, which are supposed indicate how one feels at the moment. These and many other codes are used to offset the visual and other nonverbal cues we use to understand each other in face-to-face interaction.

Being able to "converse" with someone at different times is convenient. It means we do not have to set appointments for mutually available times to meet. We can take care of business in whatever sequence suits us and from wherever we may be.

Being able to communicate quickly, in different modes, and using convenient preferences allows us to be in touch with others how and when we want. The problem (but some might call it an advantage) with distant communication is that we can avoid confrontation, according to our needs and preferences.

If we have to address conflict with another person, some might prefer to avoid doing it, or at least avoid doing it face-to-face. This may provide some protection for those in organizationally unequal positions or highly emotional circumstances.

So the effectiveness of communicating depends on accurate transmission of a message (with all of the possible glitches that can occur) and the willingness of a person to *listen*. The effective leader has learned how to communicate well. This ability to understand what others want us to understand affirms our leadership.

> "If one knows how to listen, one can learn even from those who speak badly."
>
> —Plutarch

POINTS TO PONDER

- Listening is a much-used but undertaught communication skill.
- Listening can be improved with practicing effective techniques.
- Modeling effective listening by leaders is important to placing emphasis on listening within the organization.
- Reflection is a key to assuring messages are understood—that is, communication has occurred.
- Electronic technology provides new challenges for communicating effectively.

REFERENCES

Barker, L. L. (1971). *Listening behavior*. Englewood Cliffs, NJ: Prentice-Hall.

Bolton, R. (1979). *People skills: How to assert yourself, listen to others, and resolve conflicts*. Englewood Cliffs, NJ: Prentice-Hall.

Fisher, R., Ury, W. L., & Patton, B. (2011). *Getting to yes: Negotiating agreement without giving in* (3rd ed.). New York, NY: Penguin Books.

Gilbert, M. B. (1984). Listening in the schools. In M. B. Gilbert (Ed.), *Directions in education: Perspectives for the 21st century* (pp. 57–69). Stockton, CA: University of the Pacific, Bureau of Educational Research and Field Services/Phi Delta Kappa, District II.

Gilbert, M. B. (1989). Perceptions of listening behaviors of school principals. *School Organisation, 9*, 271–282.

International Listening Association. (1996). President's perspective. *ILA Listening Post, 56,* 2–3.

Lyle, M. (1984, March). *Teaching listening skills for parents.* Presentation at the annual convention of the International Listening Association, Scottsdale, AZ.

Nichols, R., & Stevens, L. (1956). *Are you listening?* New York, NY: McGraw-Hill.

Papa, M. J., & Glenn, E. C. (1973). Listening ability and performance with new technology: A case study. *The Journal of Business Communication, 25*(4), 5–15.

Rankin, P. (1928). The importance of listening ability. *English Journal, 17,* 623–30.

Rogers, C. R. (1970). Being in relationship. *Voices The Art and Science of Psychotherapy,* 6(2), 11–19.

Steil, L. K. (1984, March). *The ILA and the certification of teachers and trainers.* Presentation at the annual convention of the International Listening Association, Scottsdale, AZ.

Steil, L. K. (1991, March). *Listening through our driving forces: A strategy for developing the complete listener.* Presentation at the 12th annual convention of the International Listening Association, Jacksonville, FL.

Steil, L. K., Barker, L. L., & Watson, K. W. (1983). *Effective listening: Key to your success.* Reading, MA: Addison-Wesley.

Steil, L. K., & Bommelje, R. K. (2002). *Listening leaders: The ten golden rules to listen, lead & succeed.* Edina, MN: Beaver Pond Press.

Tannen, D. (1990). *You just don't understand: Men and women in conversation.* New York, NY: William Morrow.

Wolff, F. I., Marsnik, N., Tacey, W., & Nichols, R. (1983). *Perceptive listening.* New York, NY: Holt, Rinehart & Winston.

Chapter Four

Communication Blueprints
Different Tools for Different Builders

People have differing communication styles and ways of processing information. Most models are based on aspects of one's preferences for taking in or giving out information, or both.

Preference for information input may be one of three modes—visual, kinesthetic (hands-on or tactile), or auditory. Personality or learning characteristics may be related to:

- communication styles and preferences, according to four scales: Extraversion-Introversion, Sensing-Intuition, Thinking-Feeling, and Judging-Perceiving (Myers 1962),
- factors: conscientiousness, agreeableness, neuroticism, openness, and extraversion (Costa & McRae, 1992)
- colors (as descriptors of preferences) (de Bono, 1985; Keirsey & Bates, 1984; Noland, 1978),
- degrees of specificity or structure (Gregorc, 1982), or
- environment or subject matter (Gardner, 1983).

In sum, we communicate depending on one or several aspects of personality and individual tendencies in life and in professional situations.

PERSONALITY MODELS

The different models all seem to focus on the preferences people have for processing information and interacting with others. Almost all of the models describe the current state of people. That is, we see various characteristics that are determined by a person's responses to an instrument or by an observation of how things are *currently*.

The identifiers charted in table 4.1 show the comparisons between the models. *Only* the Kahler (1982) model (described in greater detail below), Process Communication, indicates the current state *and* if an individual has experienced a change in preferences.

Process Communication also shows the potential a person has to interact easily and effectively with others who are different. This model provides a *toolbox* with myriad tools for different situations.

The Process Communication Model (PCM) (Kahler, 1982) describes six personality types, drawing on Transactional Analysis concepts (Berne, 1964), with historical underpinnings from Karl Jung and Alfred Adler. According to Kahler, no one personality type is better than another.

One's personality structure resembles a six-story condominium, where the first floor represents the foundation—strongest personality type—and where each remaining floor represents the other personality types in order of the strength of each. This order of personality types, generated through responses on a valid and reliable inventory (Ampaw, Gilbert & Donlan, 2013; Gilbert & Donlan, 2016; Kahler, 1982), is firmly established about age seven, and the ability to move to these different "floors" of our personality is measurable and predictable. One can access the different floors by going up or coming down in an "elevator."

Each personality type has a different set of needs, perceptions, and behaviors that influences how we interact with other and the world in which we live. This multidimensional approach is a major asset of the PCM. The *condominium* analogy is quite apt because it suggests we *own* our personality and, moreover, it is paid for—no mortgage or lien. However, it does require some maintenance. One *example* of a personality condominium is found in Figure 4.1.

The person represented by the condominium in Figure 4.1 is said to be a *Base* Thinker, with Thinker being the "ground floor". This is the strongest part of this individual's personality.

You will note that with each successive floor the amount of "furnishings" (relative energy) is equal to or less than the floor beneath it. This "energy" depicts what the individual has at his or her disposal to be able to interact with others.

For the person exemplified in Figure 4.1, there is sufficient energy to interact with Thinkers and Harmonizers, with Persisters not too far behind. Rebels, Promoters, and Imaginers would present more of a challenge.

Most people limit how they *process* reality by using only one or two of the six available floors of their personality structure. The PCM proposes that rec-

Table 4.1. Comparative Personality Indicators

Kahler	M/B	Gregorc	DeBono	McCarthy	K/B	Gardner	Costa/McCrae
Harmonizer	E*FJ	AS	Red Hat	Style One		Interpersonal	Agreeableness
Thinker	**TJ	CS	Black Hat	Style Two	Gold	Logical-Mathematical	Conscientiousness
Persister	**TJ	CS	Blue Hat	Style Two	Green	Spatial; Linguistic	Conscientiousness
Imaginer	I*TP	CR	White Hat		Blue	Intrapersonal	
Rebel	EN*P	AR	Green Hat	Style Four	Orange	Musical; Bodily-Kinesthetic	Extraversion
Promoter	*NT*	CR	Yellow Hat	Style Three		Bodily-Kinesthetic	Extraversion

Myers-Briggs (M/B) Identifiers: E= Extraverted; F= Feeling; I= Introverted; J= Judging; N= Intuitive; P= Perceptive; T= Thinking
Gregorc Delineators: A= Abstract; C= Concrete; R= Random; S= Sequential
K/B = Keirsey-Bates

Sources

Costa, P. T., Jr., & McCrae, R. R. (1992). *The NEO Personality Inventory—Revised manual*. Odessa FL: Psychological Assessment Resources.
De Bono, E. (1985). *Six thinking hats*. Toronto: Little, Brown and Co.
Gardner, H. (1983). *Frames of mind: The theory of multiple intelligences*. New York, NY: Basic Books.
Gregorc, A. (1982). *Gregorc style delineator*. Maynard, MA: Gabriel Systems, Inc.
Kahler, T. (1996). *Process Communication Model*. Little Rock, AR: Kahler Communications.
Keirsey, D., & Bates, M. (1984). *Please understand me: Character and temperament types*. Del Mar, CA: Gnosology Books.
McCarthy, B. (1980). *The 4MAT system: Teaching to learning styles with right/left mode techniques*. Barrington, IL: Excel, Inc.
Myers, I. B. (1962). *Myers-Briggs Type Indicator*. Palo Alto, CA: Consulting Psychologists Press.

ognizing diverse personality types, needs (motivators), and negative behavior (distress) sequences is the key to effective communication and success.

The words one uses indicate what one prefers. You will learn what these are as you examine the sample personalities in the following chapters. For example, Harmonizers would use feeling-laden terms: "I love your outfit." "I am so happy today." "How are you feeling?"

[Personalized profiles can be generated from an inventory validated for purposes of determining an individual's personality structure. These profiles

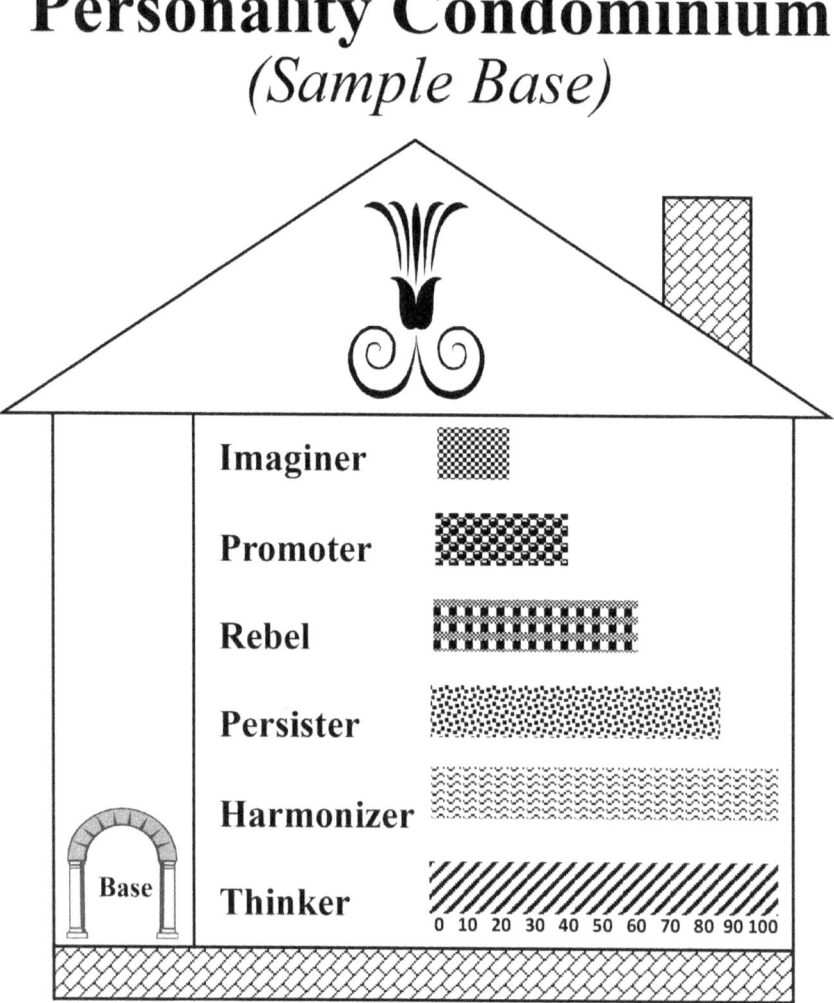

Figure 4.1. Sample Base. *Source*: Kahler Communications Inc.

include what one's motivators are, how one takes in and gives out information, and a reliable prediction of the negative behaviors a person will manifest when in distress.

This aspect of predictable distress, also the need to measure compatibility, is why the PCM has been used by National Aeronautics and Space Administration (NASA) in the selection and training of astronauts (Kahler, 1982). Other organizations that have used the Process Communication Model include Pixar, Coca-Cola, Bayer, Audi, HP, IBM, etc.]

AN OVERVIEW OF PROCESS COMMUNICATION

The following describes each personality type (Kahler, 1982, 2010):

- **Harmonizers** are *warm, compassionate, and sensitive*; they like conversation and group-oriented activities. They show their emotions, like to please, and know they are appreciated. Feelings are their forte. (30% of the North American population has Harmonizer Base personalities; mainly female—75%)
- **Thinkers** are *responsible, logical, and organized*; they think before they feel and would rather their work be recognized than appreciated personally. (25%; mainly male—75%)
- **Persisters** are *observant, conscientious, and dedicated*; they have strong beliefs about how a job should be done and definite opinions and values. (10%; mainly male—75%)
- **Rebels** are *spontaneous, creative, and playful*; they react with likes and dislikes. They need fun, attention, and active involvement. They prefer stimulating environments and prefer to interact with people who like to play. (20%; mainly female—60%)
- **Promoters** are *resourceful, adaptable, and charming*; they adapt their behavior to the situation. They need immediate rewards and exciting, stimulating activities. They prefer to be active more than feeling or thinking. (5%; mainly male—60%)
- **Imaginers** are *imaginative, reflective, and calm*; they usually are passive and are absorbed with their thoughts. They seldom initiate conversations and start withdrawing when there is too much activity around them. (10%; mainly female—60%)

The intriguing/disturbing conclusion that can be drawn from an examination of personality types is that people whose needs are not met are going to have difficulties in interacting and in meeting performance expectations. For example, a Rebel is very distractible and *needs* to have fun. If the activity is not "fun" (too repetitive or structured), the Rebel may respond, "I just don't get it," as a way of drawing others into playing with him. (In PCM parlance, this is called a "Try Hard" *Driver* [Kahler & Capers, 1974], the first degree of predictable distress.)

A supervisor who is not predisposed to spend the extra energy required to meet a Rebel's needs (or who may not have much Rebel energy to draw upon) may suppose that the Rebel is inattentive, stupid, or immature. This may mean that the Rebel may not perform as expected.

Another example of a potential communication problem may be a Harmonizer staff member assigned to a Thinker. The Harmonizer needs sensory things (like pleasing colors, aromas, or family pictures) and must feel accepted as a person by others. The Thinker is predisposed to efficiency and may see sensory things as frivolous and unimportant.

The Thinker is also task-oriented and may not have (make) the time for the pleasantries and "stroking" needed by the Harmonizer. Should the Thinker consider praising someone, that praise is likely to be couched in terms of *his psychological need* of recognition of work (Kahler, 1982)—"Good job! You've increased your target by 10%."

Since Harmonizers need unconditional recognition as people, the person might say to herself, "Why does he just only see my work? I want to be liked and appreciated as a person. Colleagues aren't just coworkers to me; they're my extended family."

Not having received the unconditional acceptance needed, the Harmonizer may make mistakes (being *driven* by a "Please You" state of mind—the first degree of distress, again). The Thinker concludes that praising does not work and begins to judge this person negatively.

THE PCM IN ACTION

Communication occurs when the receiver of a message understands the sender in the way the sender wants to be understood. The other side, *miscommunication*, is that we do not communicate when the receiver does not accept the offer or *channel* of communication (Kahler, 1979).

Responding is the capstone (see Epilogue) of most interactions—understanding the message and processing it to a response complete the communication event. In responding, the receiver becomes the sender and vice versa. Yet, it is crucial that the response match the needs and perceptions of the individuals for *communication* to occur—*saying it right*.

An example of processing the message and responding appropriately is found in the PCM through the perceptions one prefers.

Perceptions. Each personality type has different perceptions to experience the environment and the world (Kahler, 1982):

Harmonizers	emotions
Thinkers	thoughts
Persisters	opinions
Imaginers	inactions (reflections)
Rebels	reactions (likes and dislikes)
Promoters	actions

These filters or screens provide the preferences for one's views and can be heard in the terms one uses.

> Harmonizers will use emotional terms: "love," "sad," "happy," etc.
> Thinkers will be logical: "ideas," "facts," "deadlines," etc.
> Persisters will share opinions and beliefs: "important," "valuable," "committed," etc.
> Imaginers will be reflective: "It seems to me that . . ." "The ideas appear sound . . ." etc.
> Rebels will react: "I like it!" "I hate this project!" etc.
> Promoters will focus on getting things done: "Bottom line," "Go for it!" etc.

When we need or want to access different aspects of who we are because a person or situation invites us, we tap into that part of our personality that matches those perceptions.

When I want to. . .	I access my
be logical or structured	Thinker
state my opinions or values	Persister
feel or sense	Harmonizer
reflect or imagine	Imaginer
be creative or react	Rebel
act or be directive	Promoter

Most of us will prefer mostly the perception of our Base personality. Other choices are based on the amount of continual invitation and access. That is, the more frequently we tap into a perception, the more familiar it becomes to us and the more adept we are in its use. Some people do not access some of the potential perceptions much or at all.

Communication. Even if one does not know what people's personalities are, their responses will give meaningful clues into what their perceptions are. We communicate in five ways, identifiable by specific words or phrases (Kahler, 1982):

- *Intervening* offers directives, imperatives, or commands aimed at the senses (touch, smell, taste, hearing, or sight). It is very useful when people are getting "out of control"; it helps them regain their composure and is useful in emergencies—"Stop! Take a breath!" It offers a message to help the other person regain control.
- *Directing* offers a command, imperative, or directive, and another person accepts this offer rationally or logically, responding crisply as a computer would in taking the command—"Make five copies of that memo and distribute it to the staff." The focus is a simple exchange of information.
- *Requesting* involves the exchange of information, clearly and crisply—"Will you give your proposal to Bob?" The request is for information; the expectation is that the response will be simple and direct.
- *Nurturing* offers from the warm, nurturing, caring, sensitive part, inviting someone else to feel cared for—"I appreciate your being part of our office family. It's nice to see you."
- *Emoting* involves an exchange from the reactive side of each person; it helps people stay receptive, creating a non-threatening and childlike atmosphere—"Wow! You really did a super job in knocking out that project."

Each personality type has preferences for which channel will be most appropriate. Imaginers are directable, and Promoters like action (the "bottom line"); they prefer *directing*. Thinkers and Persisters are task-oriented; they prefer *requesting*. Harmonizers want to *feel* first; they prefer *nurturing*. And Rebels are driven by likes and dislikes (reactions); they prefer to communicate first through *emoting*.

Channel	Personality
Intervening	All
Directing	Imaginer
	Promoter
Requesting	Persister
	Thinker
Nurturing	Harmonizer
Emoting	Rebel

We tend to offer our own preferred communication channel predominantly (found in our personality base, or ground floor) and accompanying view of the world (perception) to others. For example, if I want to communicate and I have a Thinker base, much of what I say will be couched in terms of ideas and thoughts. If I say, "Do you *think* that is a good *idea*?" then I requested and advertised my perceptual bias of the world—thoughts. If I am addressing someone with a Harmonizer base, still I have missed that person's preference. This will be heard in a response such as "I *feel* good about it." However, the Harmonizer can move to the thinking part of her personality to communicate with the Thinker, even if that is not her preference or strongest part—but she first must have gotten energized in her strongest parts in order to be able to move.

Responses from the other types might be:

"I *believe* it is a valuable idea," for Persisters;
"I *like* it," for Rebels;
"*It's* okay," for Imaginers; and
"Okay! *Go for it!*" for Promoters.

If leaders know the proper channels and perceptions for communicating with their staff, they can help with understanding the message and encouraging the desired behavior. Here it begins to become obvious that content is not the only aspect of communicating effectively.

For example, telling a Harmonizer that the proposal is not appropriate for the organization at this time might begin with, "I am really glad that you are a member of our staff. I enjoy working with you." This will nurture the Harmonizer before, "I am sorry that we will not be able to approve your proposal now."

A Thinker supervisor would, by nature, give only the rationale (logic), but the introductory statement of personal acceptance would reinforce the relationship with an acknowledged people person, who will hear the rest of the content through nurturing filters. Therefore, communication will occur—the receiver accepting and understanding the message. Attempting to force individuals to accept a message through filters that are not theirs will result in misunderstanding and miscommunication.

I remember a PCM workshop I was facilitating with a school staff. They had all completed the PCM inventory and received their individual profiles. The focus was the basic concepts of PCM.

As with many workshops, concepts are presented intensely. If the concepts are relatively new to the participants, there is much to absorb in a short period of time.

At one point in the second day, one participant with a Persister base (belief-oriented) said she was a bit overwhelmed and asked me to "bring it down to my level." I was feeling a bit playful and knelt in front of her, asking, "Is this better?" She literally growled at me.

Someone with a lot of Rebel energy would have been energized with my playfulness, but this person was not amused. She had asked me a direct question, requesting specific information. She expected a direct answer. When she did not get it, she began to get into distress with her "You have to be perfect to be OK" driver.

It was an excellent example of miscommunication. I used it to demonstrate how I had failed to communicate—there was an offer of a message with no acceptance and in the wrong channel. (I wish I could say I had planned the interaction, but I had not.)

MOTIVATION

Needs

Each of us has needs. Abraham Maslow (1954) described them in categories from basic biological needs to higher-level psychological and social needs. Process Communication describes needs as those things that motivate us when we get them and distress us when we do not (Kahler, 1982). Each personality type has different needs. (These needs are listed here and described in further detail as we look more deeply at each personality type below.)

- **Harmonizers** need *acceptance of self* and *sensory* (satisfaction).
- **Thinkers** need *recognition for* (good) *work* and *time structure*.
- **Persisters** need *recognition for* (valuable) *work* and *conviction*.
- **Imaginers** need *solitude*.
- **Rebels** need playful *contact*.
- **Promoters** need *incidence* (short-term activities with quick payoffs).

Phase

The Base is the strongest part of one's personality structure. Those strongest aspects of each person are evident by six months of age (Kahler, 1996a; Kahler & Capers, 1974).

One's *phase* describes where each of us finds positive motivation by getting our needs met. This may be described by the personality type of our base or elsewhere in our structure.

Individuals may experience a change in *phase* and move into another part of their structure. This means that they assume the psychological needs (motivators) of that personality type under normal circumstances.

Two thirds of individuals will change their phase at least once during their lives. The dynamics that cause this change may be with or without our awareness. Phases last from two years to a lifetime, and changes occur predominantly when individuals confront and *resolve* long-term, intense distress with a particular life issue. These issues (Kahler, 1996b) are:

Harmonizers	anger
Thinkers	loss
Persisters	fear
Imaginers	autonomy
Rebels	responsibility
Promoters	bonding

How these issues are interpreted into one's experience will be described below when we look at each of the personality types individually. In a small percentage of phase changes, individuals move for positive reasons. The difference may be either pushed out of a phase or being pulled into one.

The person whose Personality Condominium is rendered in Figure 4.2 is a Thinker (Base) in a Persister Phase. The strongest part of his (mostly likely because 75% of Thinkers are male) personality involves seeing the world through thoughts, ideas, and logic. His current motivation comes from his Persister needs of *recognition of work* (as contributing in important ways) and *conviction*.

The probable reasons he changed phases (with or without his conscious awareness) were because of resolving long-term distress first with loss (the issue for Thinkers) and then with anger (having *staged* through his Harmonizer). When he changed might not be pinpointed in time, but it is obvious that his preferences and motivation are different.

His friends and associates have probably noticed and commented how he seems more committed. He dresses differently—more according to the "rules" and less for comfort (as he might have dressed in his Harmonizer phase). He will interact more with regard for what others believe than for how they feel; however, results are still important to him.

Under normal circumstances in slight distress (not getting the work recognition and conviction he *now* needs), he will focus on what is wrong, rather than what is right. If his needs continue to be unmet, he may preach or crusade and seem to attack others for their lack of commitment.

A Persister Phase person found himself overcommitted in terms of his job responsibilities, extracurricular activities, and the scheduling of his doctoral courses during one summer. He wrote a long note to a faculty member berating her for not understanding how busy working students are at the end of the school year and how she had failed to apprise him of the summer schedule early enough. He went further to say that he would do all he could to get the schedule changed so future groups of students would be accommodated better.

His failure to plan carefully or manage his time better was overlooked in deference to someone else's not "being perfect" and furthermore not understanding part-time students' needs.

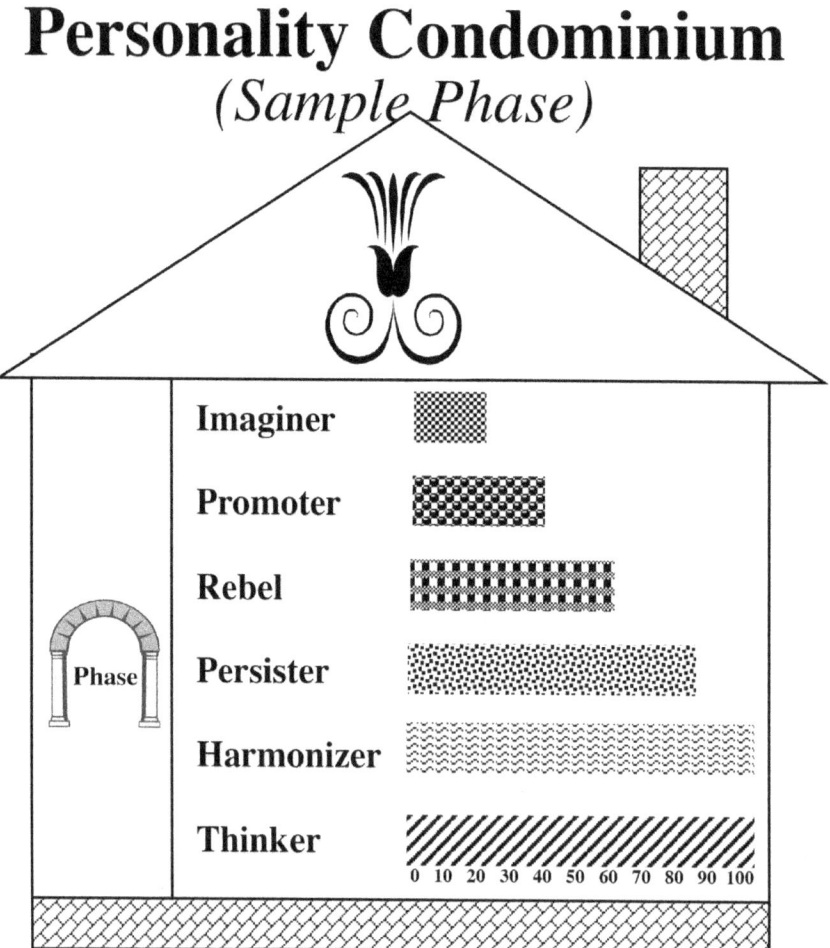

Figure 4.2.　Sample Phase. *Source*: Kahler Communications Inc.

These are both examples of the first- and second-degree distress for Persisters. First, his advisor was not OK because she was not perfect, and second, he preached at her for not being more considerate, then "threatening" to crusade for better conditions.

If the person shown in Figure 4.2 experiences severe distress, he will retreat back to his strongest "floor," his base. Here, the distress will be seen in his attempts to regain control by not delegating to others to do their part and his becoming critical about fairness, responsibility, finances, etc.—the signs of a Thinker trying to get recognition for his good work, albeit negatively.

The unspoken message is, "If I work harder and longer, surely someone will acknowledge my good work." Taking on more work can be enervating and unlikely to fulfill his needs.

The predictable nature of Process Communication is its value to understanding others. This understanding leads to effective communication.

INTERACTION STYLES

We interact with others according to how we prefer others interact with us. Each Personality Type shows the preferences of interacting autocratically, democratically, benevolently, or in a *laissez-faire* manner (Kahler, 1982). These behaviors are typical, predictable, and habitual. Choosing another style requires that the effective leader move to another's *frame of preference.*

Because of their predominance for base strengths in Harmonizer, Persister, or Thinker, leaders will also prefer either *benevolent* or *democratic* interaction (administrative) styles. That is, the way that they choose to relate to others will be either caring and person-oriented, or will be task-oriented and designed to invite the participation of others in activities or decisions.

Those with whom they have the most difficulty communicating will prefer either an *autocratic* (directive) or *laissez-faire* (non-directive) style. These interaction preferences are listed in Table 4.2 (from Kahler, 1982, adapted with permission).

DAY-TO-DAY OPERATIONS

Staff are quite capable, under *positive* conditions, of using the behaviors and preferences of more than one of the personality types. So, the leader can offer instructions for Harmonizers—group activities—and have most staff succeed. (Note that neither the leader nor staff need to be base Harmonizers for this to happen.)

Table 4.2. Interaction Styles

Interaction Style	Characteristics	Advantages	Disadvantages
Autocratic	Commands; directives; direct responses	Useful for those who require direction or structure	Does not invite group interaction or upward feedback
Democratic	Group participation; interaction between/among others	Encourages self-paced growth; increases group cohesion; enhances morale	Does not provide enough structure for those who need it, or who lack knowledge and understanding
Benevolent	Belonging; caring; nurturing; accepting	Works well with those who need unconditional acceptance	Possibly seen as invasion of privacy, or personal trespass on professional relationships
Laissez-Faire	Nondirective	Works well for self-styled people, inviting independence and creativity	Does not provide direction and structure

But what if the leader offers instructions in only one mode? We can predict with certainty which staff will lose energy and begin their failure patterns.

PCM is very precise. We can anticipate the actual behaviors of a particular type of staff member *before* he or she fails.

Using this information, the leader can intervene early and invite staff back into their success patterns. What makes this work is that staff prefer to succeed and will cooperate with a leader who appears to understand them, accept them, and accommodate their communication preferences sincerely.

The PCM is simple, yet comprehensive and thorough, covering interaction styles, communication preferences, psychological needs, physical environments, perceptions, driver behaviors, failure patterns, and failure mechanisms. At first blush, the Model may appear difficult to understand because of its comprehensiveness. However, successful leaders find they are already using some of the information, and they can add new strategies one piece at a time. The best news is that it works, providing ways for all people to succeed and remain positive.

BENEFITS

It is important to understand that the PCM focuses predominantly on **process** —not content—and process is a more challenging focus and takes longer to change. The exciting result is that changing process can relate to all aspects of an organization. The benefits are both tangible and intangible. The most tangible benefit is smoother flow of information—of course, this may translate into revenue.

The greatest intangible benefit is more effective communication throughout the organization—administrators and staff, staff and clients, and staff with each other. Moreover, this benefit carries over into personal lives, where communication becomes more effective between the individuals and their families and others.

CONCLUSION

Changing the processes that we use in an organization is more difficult and takes longer than changing what we know—and that might not be effective. Many managers subscribe to the notion that staff must function within specific (singular) behavior patterns in order for them to succeed. This limited perspective ignores the diversity of needs we confront as leaders.

We need to take the time and find sufficient energy to deal effectively with the differences that confront us. Understanding ourselves and others, knowing what negative behaviors mean and what to do about them in the organization, while focusing more and more on **how** we communicate, can have profound positive consequences.

WHO AM I?

With all of the information presented in this chapter, you may be wondering who you are—that is, what are your communication characteristics and preferences?

If you see the world through, and...	If you are energized by...	You have strong tendencies as a...
Thoughts and ideas	Recognition for work and time structure	**Thinker**
Feelings and emotions	Acceptance of who you are and sensory	**Harmonizer**
Beliefs, values, and opinions	Recognition of your valuable work and conviction	**Persister**
Reflections and imagination	Being alone and solitary	**Imaginer**
Likes and dislikes	Playful contact	**Rebel**
Actions	Lots of activities in short bursts with quick payoffs	**Promoter**

POINTS TO PONDER

- People have varying characteristics of six personality types.
- The aspects of the predominant personalities determine how individuals behave.
- The base personality describes your strongest tendencies, especially perceptual preferences.
- The phase personality describes how you are motivated—what you need.
- You generally try to get your needs met positively.
- When you do not get your needs met positively, you will attempt to get the same needs met negatively in very predictable ways, seen in varying levels of distress.
- You communicate easiest with those who are similar to you. Those who are (very) different present greater challenges.
- Effective communication occurs when a message is offered and accepted using an appropriate style.

REFERENCES

Ampaw, F. D., Gilbert, M. B., & Donlan, R. A. (2013). Verifying the validity and reliability of the Personality Pattern Inventory: Preliminary results. *Journal of Process Communication, 1*(1), 27–46.

Berne, E. (1964). *Games people play: The psychology of human relationships.* New York: NY Grove Press.

Costa, P. T., Jr., & McRae, R. R. (1992). *The NEO Personality Inventory—Revised manual.* Odessa, FL: Psychological Assessment Resources.

De Bono, E. (1985). *Six thinking hats*. Toronto: Little, Brown and Co.

Gardner, H. (1983). *Frames of mind: The theory of multiple intelligences*. New York, NY: Basic Books.

Gilbert, M. B., & Donlan, R. A. (with Parr, J.). (2016). Personality Pattern Inventory. In V. Zeigler-Hill & T. K. Shackelford (Eds.), *Encyclopedia of personality and individual differences* (pp. 1–5). Online: Springer International Publishing AG, doi:10.1007/978-3-319-28099-8_60-1

Gregorc, A. (1982). *Gregorc style delineator*. Maynard, MA: Gabriel Systems, Inc.

Johnson, D. W. (1993). *Reaching out: Interpersonal effectiveness and self-actualization* (5th ed.). Englewood Cliffs, NJ: Prentice-Hall.

Kahler, T. (1979). *Process therapy in brief*. Little Rock, AR: Human Development Publications.

Kahler, T. (1982). *Personality Pattern Inventory validation studies*. Little Rock, AR: Kahler Communications, Inc.

Kahler, T. (1996a). *Personality Pattern Inventory*. Little Rock, AR: Kahler Communications, Inc.

Kahler, T. (1996b). *The Key to Me seminar*. Little Rock, AR: Kahler Communications, Inc.

Kahler, T. (2010). *Process Communication management semimar*. Little Rock, AR: Kahler Communications, Inc.

Kahler, T., & Capers, H. (1974). The miniscript. *Transactional Analysis Journal, 4*(1), 26–42.

Keirsey, D., & Bates, M. (1984). *Please understand me: Character and temperament types*. Del Mar, CA: Gnosology Books.

Maslow, A. H. (1954). *Motivation and personality*. New York, NY: Harper.

Myers, I. B. (1962). *Myers-Briggs Type Indicator*. Palo Alto, CA: Consulting Psychologists Press.

Noland, J. R. (1978). *Personalysis*. St. Paul, MN: Communication Development, Inc.

Stansbury, P. (1990). *Abridged test-retest reliability study for the PPI*. Little Rock, AR: Kahler Communications, Inc.

WHAT'S TO COME

The next section will describe six *pure* personality types, recognizing that no one is singular but a composite of each of these personalities in varying degrees. You will meet: Barbara, Alfred, Matthew, Dorothy, Angie, and Doug. Each person will be seen in both positive and negative ways, all of which are predictable.

To emphasize: you will never meet any of the people as they are described exclusively. What you will encounter are people who will show you preferences and behaviors of one of the six people you are about to meet. In the real world, you may notice that people change. When this occurs, you will see another aspect of who they are, but they are still the same people.

Following the narrative description of each person will be a profile including the following components:

- Character Strengths
- Perceptual Preference
- Psychological Needs
- Administrative Style
- Driver
- Failure Mechanism
- Life Issue

Section II

BUILDING BLOCKS: PURE PERSONALITY TYPES

PURE PERSONALITY TYPES

You are about to meet six people—Barbara, Alfred, Matthew, Dorothy, Angie, and Doug. Each is presented as a *pure* personality type—that is, you will see each person as if there are no components of other personalities.

As you understand the unique characteristics of each person, you will begin to see the different aspects of personalities—which are combined in each of us in varying degrees of strength (as shown in the sample condominims earlier). Please note that we are combinations of all of these personalities. We have preferences for communicating and the ability to shift to other positions when invited and *if we are OK* ourselves.

You will speculate about yourself—wondering what your Base is, and in what Phase you are currently. The description of each person will give you good hints about yourself. The purpose is that you be able to understand others as you interact with them in your professional and personal life. (See also "Who Am I?" in the previous chapter.)

PROBLEMS SITUATIONS AND SUGGESTIONS FOR RESOLUTION

Following your introduction to each personality, you will be presented with problems situations that demonstrate the *predictable* distress of each personality type, or situations that may foster distress if not handled *deftly*. You will encounter a key actor showing negative behaviors or presenting an important perspective for you to ponder. These behaviors indicate that the individual lacks positive motivation—that is, his or her needs are not being met positively. *Symptoms for Consideration* will be offered, followed by *Suggestions for Action*.

Chapter Five

Pure Harmonizer: Barbara

Barbara ("Bobbie" to her numerous friends) is a *compassionate, sensitive,* and *warm* person. She's described as a Harmonizer—a very giving person. Her parents marveled at her warmth and caring nature from the time she was quite young.

She wants to help others become healthy people emotionally and be able to help others. Barbara's life is filled with sensual things.

Her home is warm and inviting. It is decorated to appeal to the senses—potpourri, flowers, and other fragrant things, soft and comfortable places to sit, and earth-tone colors throughout. Her office has reminders of the precious and familiar things in her life—photographs of her family (including her special friend, Ernie, a cat she named after her favorite Sesame Street character), soft petit-point pillows, and a wall hanging her father got on a trip to Africa.

She sees the world through her emotions. She wants to know how others feel and that they are OK. "How do you *feel*?" is a question she is likely to ask, and she will be very attentive to the answer, focusing on emotions.

She is most comfortable when she can interact with others—individually or in groups. She prefers to have people around her and work closely with them. She is motivated almost always with a thought of what she perceives others may need.

Barbara is likely to offer and give (and receive) hugs often. She may touch others when talking with them, especially if she knows her touch is welcome. *Warm fuzzies,* things that invite people to feel good, are her preference—to give and receive.

Barbara needs *acceptance of self*—who she is—and *sensory satisfaction.* She needs to know she is appreciated and wanted, and she takes advantage of opportunities to experience things that appeal to her senses.

She can never be around too many people. At social gatherings, she would be sure everyone was comfortable, fed, and in a "good place," even if she were not hosting the gathering. You might find her in the kitchen, serving food or drink, or being sure that everyone has been introduced to everyone else.

She will try to help those who are having any type of difficulty—from fixing a balky zipper to smoothing out a stormy relationship. She is highly empathic—to the point of mirroring someone else's emotions or what he "should" be feeling. She is in her element if she can support or aid others.

Barbara will dress in comfortable and visually pleasing clothes. The fabrics she chooses will feel good to the touch, especially hers. Her hair will be arranged nicely and with care.

She will wear her favorite fragrances. If she has only one favorite, it will be her "signature smell."

She prefers to work with people who accept her unconditionally—either as a staff member or administrator. She works well with people.

As an administrator, it would be important to Barbara to work in a people-oriented situation. She might choose to be a counselor or perhaps director of personnel.

Working in a position that was highly task-oriented without much personal contact would weaken her emotionally. (She would be the archetypal *1,9 manager*, using the Blake and Mouton *Managerial Grid* [1985]. She would show a very high degree of concern for people and a lower degree of concern for production.)

Barbara is likely to remark about how pleasant someone else looks or the fragrance she (or he) is wearing. She will focus almost exclusively on the positives of other people and is unlikely to criticize them face-to-face.

However, she might ask a colleague if something is wrong with someone she senses is having difficulty—at home or at work. She will want to know if there is something she can do "to make it better." While her own needs are important, sometimes she will set them aside when she *feels* someone else *needs* her.

She is prone to using "smiley faces" and flowery handwriting, and is very attentive to others. She is likely to bring home-baked cookies or muffins to the lounge or to staff meetings. Most of her actions are meant to "make" others feel good.

(The perception of "making others feel good" is one of the *myths* of interaction [Kahler, 1978]. We cannot force others to feel a certain way, nor can others control how we feel. We have a choice; however, certain things in our environment may be very compelling for how we choose to feel. For example, when confronted with sad stories, Harmonizers may also *feel* sad and tear up. Others may not.)

Barbara's predominant administrative style is *benevolent*. She will work with others in a way designed for them to be comfortable and welcome.

She is person-oriented and focuses more on people than thoughts or tasks. The feelings of others are most important to her. Her presumption is that when people "feel" good, they perform better and interact more effectively. Her style is to foster a sense of belonging in others by accepting them.

She will communicate predominantly in a *nurturing* way. Her words and tones are caring and warm. She will attempt to comfort others as a nurturing parent would. She wants them to know that "I really appreciate you, and I look forward to being with you. I want to help you feel good."

If she has an unfinished issue in life, it is likely to be *anger*. Her need for acceptance of herself and to accept others overrides giving herself permission to be angry.

This difficulty with being angry or expressing anger in appropriate ways is distressful for her: "If I express my anger at you, I will have hurt your feelings and/or you will reject me. Therefore, I will please you and hold in my anger" (Kahler, 1996).

If Barbara is unable to get her *acceptance of self* or *sensory satisfaction* needs met positively, she will begin to show predictable driver (the first indicator of distress) behaviors by overadapting in an attempt to *please* others. (Distress behaviors or patterns are an attempt to get the same needs met *negatively.*) She is moving into an "I'm not OK—you're OK" position. She will show this posture with or without her awareness. She will overadapt to situations or people: *"Could you . . . maybe . . . take, sorta, a careful look at this?"*

If the *Please You* driver does not allow Barbara to attain what she needs (and it usually does not), she will, again predictably, slip into second-degree distress. Here she will feel sad, worried, anxious, or confused.

She will give off *warning signals* of lacking assertiveness, laughing at herself, or acting "stupid." It may seem as if she is wearing a "Kick me!" sign.

If her needs are not met over time, she may look different. She may not be as careful in her dress or appearance as she is usually, even to the point of being unkempt.

She dons a *Drooper* mask and appears victimized. She may appear depressed. If her distress continues for a long period, she may even become hysterical at times.

Her *failure mechanism* is making mistakes, which is *not* related to her intelligence or her competence. These warning signs suggest that Barbara is not motivated positively.

She needs to arrange to be nurtured unconditionally either by herself or a warm and caring person in her life—someone who will let her know she is important to him or her and who will listen to how she feels. Barbara also

56   Chapter Five

needs to nurture herself sensually—with a bubble bath, new clothes, or spending time with people who like her for herself and have no ulterior motives.

If Barbara works with a supervisor who does not understand her *needs*, she is likely to request a transfer to a more nurturing environment or she may seek employment elsewhere. These potential alternatives may not be true options, because Barbara is likely to be highly place-bound. That is, she is not likely to pick up and move easily.

She may be a secondary wage earner in her household, or she may be inextricably tied to her location or environment with a large circle of family and friends. As a result, she may stay in distress and be less productive in both her professional and personal lives.

Barbara's Profile	
Character Strengths:	Compassionate, sensitive, warm
Perceptual Preference:	Emotions
Motivational Needs:	Acceptance of self; sensory satisfaction
Channel:	Nurturative
Administrative Style:	Benevolent
Driver:	Please you
Failure Mechanism:	Makes mistakes; invites criticism
Life Issue:	Anger

(Adapted with permission from Kahler, T. [1995, 1996].)

PROBLEM SITUATION

Barbara has been an administrative aide in your organization for 12 years. Recently, you have noticed that she is often late, appears slovenly, and turns in sloppy and inaccurate reports. Her enthusiasm for her job and her caring for others also seem to have diminished.

These behaviors are different from what you have seen previously. You have heard that she is having some difficulty at home. As her supervisor, you are concerned.

Symptoms for Consideration

Barbara's behavior has changed dramatically. Her *appearance* and the *mistakes* she is making indicates she is in Harmonizer distress. She has not arranged to have her *acceptance of self* and *sensory* needs met—apparently both at home and at work. She has probably shown a lot of "Please you" behaviors by attempting to overadapt to people and situations, and has been unsuccessful in getting her needs met through accommodating others. She is inviting criticism in her negative posture and has assumed a "Kick me!" stance.

Suggestions for Action

- Tell her how pleased you are to see her each day. Let her know that her presence brightens the lives of others and adds to organization.
- Ask her how her family is. Listen to her empathically if she chooses to "unload" with you about any problems she may be having at home. (Note: Be sure you have the time to offer her, or set up some time for her to talk with you. This may be accomplished best at the end of the work day, in case her catharsis leaves her emotionally drained.)
- Appreciate *her* publicly at a faculty meeting. (Note: As you express your appreciation of her, focus on her as a person, not on what she has accomplished. For example, say *"Barbara is one of the most caring people I know. The organizational family means a great deal to her."*)
- Support her unconditionally, even though she may be having problems. If you have the authority to do so, invite her to take some days off to do something to pamper herself, thereby regaining the necessary energy to move her from her distress.
- If you do not perceive it as favoritism, give her a small gift that indicates you appreciate her—a "Big Hug Mug," a package of potpourri, or something else that will appeal to her senses. (Male administrators may want to consider if these small pieces of appreciation may be perceived as inappropriate, given current concerns of sexual harassment.)

(Adapted with permission from Kahler, T. [1982, 1995].)

REFERENCES

Blake, R. R., & Mouton, J. S. (1985). *The Managerial Grid III: A new look at the classic that has boosted productivity and profits for thousands of corporations worldwide.* Houston, TX: Gulf Publishing Co.

Kahler, T. (1978). *TA revisited.* Little Rock, AR: Human Development Publications.

Kahler, T. (1982). *Personality Pattern Inventory studies.* Little Rock, AR: Kahler Communications, Inc.

Kahler, T. (1995). *The Process Education seminar.* Little Rock, AR: Kahler Communications, Inc.

Kahler, T. (1996). *The Key to Me seminar.* Little Rock, AR: Kahler Communications, Inc.

Chapter Six

Pure Thinker: Alfred

Alfred is a *logical, responsible,* and *organized* person. He recognizes his strong ability to organize activities, to put concepts into logical sequences, and to operate in a timely and focused fashion. His life is structured into sensible and time-oriented blocks. His home is highly functional—everything in its place and a place for everything.

His office is arranged for efficiency. His desk is orderly and usually clean and uncluttered at the end of each day. His workspace is designed so he can get to needed equipment and files easily.

His computer is state-of-the-art, with a fast processor and a large amount of memory and file storage capacity (probably more than he will ever use, but one never knows). He has backup, security, and power-surge protection to prevent tampering and any kind of information loss.

Alfred (never "Al") prefers to do things only once. His office has a large array of certificates, plaques, and awards, attesting to his accomplishments and hard work.

Alfred experiences the world through his thoughts, ideas, and logic. He expects others to think clearly and be responsible for themselves and for their work. He does not "suffer fools easily."

He prefers to work alone or one-on-one. He is a self starter—that is, he does not need to be stimulated or motivated much by others.

When he asks a question, he expects a direct answer—one that responds to what he asked. When working with others, he wants them to be prepared. He admires independent thinking.

Alfred works best in structured situations—areas that are highly predictable and that have logical boundaries. As an administrator, he is likely to focus on order—in people and things. Rules are established for order. Discipline and orderly procedures would be paramount in any venture he might oversee.

His reports are neat, precise, and on time. He does not need to make all the decisions, but he would insist that decisions be made rationally and sensibly.

Alfred needs *recognition for (good) work* and *time structure.* He wants to know that others acknowledge his hard work and clear thinking.

His life, both personal and professional, is orderly and timely. He can "play," but only if he has finished his work first. The "games" he chooses usually have clear rules and outcomes. He is likely to gravitate to those things that are precise—chess, checkers, bridge, puzzles, knowledge or trivia games, etc.

He has difficulty with amorphous things—before he starts, he wants to be sure he knows the objective and will move definitively in that direction. He maps his routes before he begins—whether he is traveling or planning for organizational change.

His schedule tends not to be overbooked, insofar as he can schedule all he has to do. Unscheduled intrusions are bothersome; he prefers people to make appointments (and keep them). He does "schedule" unencumbered time to be out and about—managing by wandering around (Peters & Austin, 1985).

Arriving at work at approximately the same time and before things become too busy, Alfred gets into each day in predictable fashion—returning phone calls, checking his electronic and postal mail, working with his secretary on correspondence and other areas, etc.

He understands that things are not always orderly and structured, so he does what he can to control those things he can. He works best when things go as planned.

Alfred will acknowledge a job well done. He focuses on the degree of accomplishment and precise or accurate work. For things done particularly well, he might send a letter or a certificate.

He would use plaques or trophies for noteworthy outcomes and present them at a formal assembly. He is not likely to be effusive in rewarding things done well, but he will be sure that others understand the importance of working hard and well. (As Barbara would manage in the *1,9* Blake-Mouton style, Alfred would be a very strong *9,1* manager, with a high degree of concern for completed tasks and a lower degree of concern for people. His focus would be on the work.)

Being *democratic* is Alfred's predominant administrative style. He subscribes strongly to principles of group participation in decision making in the proper context.

He will encourage interaction between and among others, solicit feedback, and foster independent thinking. He thinks this style will encourage goal-oriented people to grow at their own pace, will increase group cohesion, and will enhance morale because of a focus on common goals (Kahler, 1982).

Alfred will use a *requesting* style in communicating with others and prefers it be used with him. His main objective is the receiving and sharing of information, usually related to getting the work done: "What do you think our options are?"

If Alfred has a life issue to resolve, it is likely to be *grief.* He may experience long-term, intense distress with a focus on what might be lost if clear thinking and predictable schedules are not the order of the day—"If I don't do the thinking for you, then something bad will happen. Therefore, I will be perfect and not make any mistakes . . . and as long as I am critical or you're not thinking clearly, I can avoid my loss" (Kahler, 1996).

If Alfred is not able to get his *recognition for work* and *time structure* needs met positively, he will show the predictable *"be perfect"* driver behaviors—pulling back on delegation of tasks and taking on more work for himself: *"If I work harder and longer, then people will recognize my good work."*

He may make an overqualified statement as an indicator of his distress: *"I am not exactly, precisely sure that is the option we should consider."* If his distress (lack of needs fulfillment) continues, he will attempt to overcontrol others. The warning signs are his being easily frustrated with those who do not think the same or clearly, and "attacking" others around issues of money, order, and responsibility.

This "attacking" is likely to spill over into his personal life with his spouse and his children. He will have difficulty understanding how people can get through life without clear thinking, how irrational or non-rational behavior can be acceptable, or why others do not or cannot see the logic of how things can go smoothly if being responsible and thinking clearly guide your actions.

The more Alfred stays in distress, the longer he will work—foregoing recreation, vacations, retirement. His absence from others who need his presence may cause them distress (especially if he is married to a caring Harmonizer). He thinks he is working for them, and does not realize that he is trying to get his own needs met by working longer and harder—not being recognized for his work.

If Alfred works with a supervisor who does not understand his *needs,* he is likely to do "battle" around thinking issues—not thinking clearly, making "silly" mistakes, being irresponsible. He would have difficulty working with someone who did not recognize his work, detail, or structure. His distress might come from disagreement with his ideas or failure to focus on issues needing to be addressed.

	Alfred's Profile
Character Strengths:	Logical, responsible, organized
Perceptual Preference:	Thoughts
Motivational Needs:	Recognition for (good) work; time structure
Administrative Style:	Democratic
Channel:	Requestive
Driver:	Be perfect
Failure Mechanism:	Overcontrols
Life Issue:	Grief

(Adapted with permission from Kahler, T. [1996].)

PROBLEM SITUATION

Alfred is a program specialist who has been on the job for 20 years and who is retiring at year's end. He has begun to take it upon himself to criticize other members of the staff about their performance of their job responsibilities, even though he serves in a staff capacity with no supervisory responsibilities.

He had been given more and more authority for discretionary action for programmatic affairs over the years, leading to a somewhat intimidating demeanor, especially for the newer staff members. He is critical about punctuality (both for arrival at work and for assignments and reports), how activities are supervised (especially with reports of monies collected), the way in which materials and supplies are requested by the staff, and other similar instances.

Symptoms for Consideration

Alfred is demonstrating Thinker distress—picky about details and time. He expects others to think clearly so that things will go smoothly. If they do not, he will take on more and more, because only he knows how to do what needs to be done—and he can do "it" faster and more efficiently.

His distress is occasioned by his not getting his Thinker needs met—*recognition for work* and *time structure*. To motivate him, you, as his supervisor, might consider how to move from negative to positive needs satisfaction.

Suggestions for Action

- Intervene into his distress by acknowledging that he is working well (if, indeed, he is): "Good job!" "You work very efficiently." "Your ideas about how to get things done are very sensible."
- Write him a note acknowledging his work, or present him with a Certificate of Accomplishment.

- Give him thoughtful problems to solve that relate to his areas of responsibility—"Will you suggest how we might rethink distributing supplies?"
- Let him know time frames for projects as he is assigned them, or ask him how long it is expected for him to complete a task.

(Adapted with permission from Kahler, T. [1982, 1996].)

REFERENCES

Blake, R. R., & Mouton, J. S. (1985). *The Managerial Grid III: A new look at the classic that has boosted productivity and profits for thousands of corporations worldwide.* Houston, TX: Gulf Publishing Co.

Kahler, T. (1982). *Process Communication Model: A contemporary model for organizational development.* Little Rock, AR: Kahler Communications, Inc.

Kahler, T. (1996). *The Key to Me seminar.* Little Rock, AR: Kahler Communications, Inc.

Peters, T., & Austin, N. (1985). *A passion for excellence: The leadership difference.* New York, NY: Random House.

Chapter Seven

Pure Persister: Matthew

Matthew is a *conscientious, dedicated,* and *observant* person. His career was guided by what he believed is important and valuable for people to know. He focuses on things that support his beliefs and values. He is very interested in politics, religion, and current events. His home is arrayed with books, pictures, and sayings that relate to his belief system. He believes his name shows the strength of his convictions and prefers to be called "Matthew," rather than "Matt."

Matthew experiences the world through his beliefs and opinions. He gravitates toward people, issues, and situations that affirm his values. As with Alfred, Matthew prefers to work alone or one-on-one. When he asks a question, he expects a direct answer—one that corresponds to what he asked.

When working with others, he wants them to know what they are doing, but, even more, he wants them to understand the importance of what they are doing—both for the current situation and for the long term. He will discuss issues and will listen to opposing points of view, accepting them only if his position has been accepted.

On issues presented in a forum in which he is an observer—such as the newspaper—he may offer an opposing point of view (e.g., letter to the editor) on a topic of deep concern to him. His zeal for causes and ideas important to him (usually politics, religion, or current events) is admirable—but can occasionally get in the way if he does not get his needs met.

Matthew gravitates to positions where he would be able to air his position and opinions. He focuses on the importance of concepts and how they contribute to the overall scheme of things.

He emphasizes doing what is right, in an orderly way, and because "society" could not function without rules of behavior. He needs *recognition for (valuable) work* and *conviction.* That is, he needs to have affirmed that his work is important and that others respect his belief system.

He, too, can "play" but only if he has finished his work first. The rules of "life" must be observed before "frivolous" things can be done or allowed. He is his own taskmaster and may become impatient if others direct him. He would prefer to be asked to take on an assignment or do a task.

Like Alfred, he finds his motivation from within, but he might also be motivated more readily by people or issues related to his belief system. He approaches his job with a sense of what is important to the mission of the organization. For example, he might choose to work on a grant proposal for a new program strategy rather than complete a periodic intra-organizational report. The report would be completed on time, but Matthew would see it as part of *"administrivia,"* the busy work to be done. He acknowledges that some people "color outside the lines," but his position is that lines are there for a purpose.

He dresses as he believes one ought, given his position and rank in the organization. He does not insist that others dress similarly, but approaches those who do so more approvingly. Staff who are untidy or who dress in a way he considers to be "careless" will get at least a mental "tsk tsk" from him.

As a leader, Matthew will not go overboard in recognizing good work because it is "what people *ought* to do." For exceptional merit, he would make a public acclamation of the valuable service of the individual and present the person with a framed print of one of his favorite sayings or a book subscribing to his beliefs.

Like Alfred, Matthew's preferred administrative style is *democratic.* He believes that staff members involved in decisions, especially those they have to implement, ought to participate to some degree in the making of those decisions.

At times, however, he may become parental on an important decision and make the decision himself, even if there is benefit to involving others. He might justify that position by saying that others did not have enough information or experience. This rationalization might cover up a *fear* that the wrong approach might be advocated. (He, as Alfred, would tend to the *9,1* style, focusing more on the work, which he believes is more important than the person.)

Matthew prefers to communicate *requestively.* He usually seeks information in his interchanges with others.

He may also ask for justification of a position he does not understand or, more likely, a position with which he disagrees: "Why do you believe we ought to do that?" He might become more parental with, "Do you mean to tell me . . . ?" This might be his way of opening a conversation that will focus on why someone else's position is wrong and untenable—in his mind.

If Matthew has a life issue to resolve, it is likely to be *fear*. He may experience long-term intense distress with a focus on what might happen if strong values and the "right" beliefs are not guideposts for action—"If I don't make sure you believe the right way and do the right things, then something bad will happen. Therefore, I expect you to be perfect and not make any mistakes and, as long as I am preaching at you, I can avoid my own fears" (Kahler, 1996).

If he does not get his *recognition for work* or *conviction* needs met positively, he will assume a parental *be perfect* driver position—focusing on what was done wrong, instead of affirming what was done correctly.

He may ask an overqualifying question: *"What exactly, precisely do you mean by that?"* If Matthew's distress continues, he will become crusading or "preachy." The warning signals are either his being frustrated with those who do not believe as he does, or his being overly critical or suspicious of others.

This distress may carry over to his personal life. He may become picky with his spouse about the way the house looks or that small aspect of a meal that did not quite work. He will expect his children to excel and "fuss" at them for the incorrect (what he might interpret as careless) responses on their homework or tests. He will go on and on about the value of an education and the importance of doing well.

When he is in distress, no one in Matthew's life, including him, can escape his criticism. His insistence that others *be perfect* can be damaging to his relationships, sometimes with dire consequences—divorce, or children who gravitate into dangerous situations, such as drugs or other behaviors that are sure to garner their father's disapproval.

If Matthew works with a supervisor whose belief system is different from his, he is likely to take that person to task on critical organizational issues, even at the risk of his job. However, because managers tend to be *based* in strong beliefs, Matthew is likely to find himself among colleagues who prefer to experience the world through their values and opinions more often than not.

	Matthew's Profile
Character Strengths:	Conscientious, dedicated, observant
Perceptual Preference:	Beliefs
Motivational Needs:	Recognition for (valuable) work; conviction
Administrative Style:	Democratic
Channel:	Requestive
Driver:	You should be perfect
Failure Mechanism:	Crusades
Life Issue:	Fear

(Adapted with permission from Kahler, T. [1996].)

PROBLEM SITUATION

Matthew, an experienced manager of an innovative and successful program, has approached you with an idea to set up an expansion to deal with some of the more pressing health issues he believes relate to his staff. You had encouraged him to write a proposal outlining the problems, a plan to address the problems, and a budget. He has presented you with a plan to provide a number of different services, including abortion counseling, HIV intervention, etc. He has justified these services by citing the rising rates of sexually transmitted diseases and unwanted pregnancies. Because of the very sensitive nature of these issues and the negative impact this plan is likely to have on the organization, you are inclined to reject the proposal.

Symptoms for Consideration

Matthew has been encouraged to develop a sensitive project, one he *believes* is important. Whether or not you approve the project is inconsequential to keeping Matthew motivated and focused on the mission of the organization. His strong *opinions and values* indicate his Persister nature.

He needs acceptance of these *convictions* and *recognition for* his *work*. (Note that acceptance of convictions does not mean you agree with him; only that you acknowledge his beliefs. Do not argue with him about whether his beliefs or opinions are right or wrong.) If you reject the project without ample explanation or justification, you are likely to see Matthew preach or crusade about the importance of dealing with such critical issues facing all staff.

Suggestions for Action

- Accept his proposal as it is written. Thank him for his hard work in developing a project so obviously important to him, and for believing in the welfare of his staff. His having heard that, you may tell him that the way in which he has proposed dealing with the situation is not going to be approved by the board at this time (if that is your assessment). Invite him to raise the issue again at another time—be specific as to when you will be ready to consider it (six months, next year, etc.).
- Commend his overall work in a letter or with some public recognition (including sending on the acknowledgment to the appropriate media).
- Recognize his dedication to the organization and his staff, when you have occasion to meet with him or contact him.
- Let him know what you admire and respect about him, especially as they may relate to his beliefs and convictions.

- Appoint him as chair of a committee to study the incidence of sexually transmitted diseases and unwanted pregnancies of all staff in the organization. Let him know that the committee's work and recommendations will be tantamount to reconsideration of his proposal.

(Adapted with permission from Kahler, T. [1996].)

REFERENCE

Kahler, T. (1996). *The advanced Process Communication seminar.* Little Rock, AR: Kahler Communications, Inc.

Chapter Eight

Pure Imaginer: Dorothy

Dorothy is an *imaginative, reflective,* and *calm* person. She wanted a regular job with an established routine. Becoming a data archivist met that desire.

Her life focuses inwardly. She prefers to reflect on things and issues and to envision what possibilities lie before her. Her home is functional and uncluttered. She has what she needs but is not prone to frills or anything overly done.

Dorothy experiences the world through her imagination and reflections. She prefers to be alone and work undisturbed. She is very good at doing repetitive tasks. Routines allow her to do her job with few interruptions or redirection.

When she is asked a question or for information, she tends to respond directly and to the point. She is unlikely to embellish or elaborate on a response unless directed to do so. When working with others, she will provide the structure or template for the activity and give them room to work. She may encourage a discussion of issues but is unlikely to engage in the discussion herself to any great extent.

Her reticence to interact to any great extent might give others the impression that she is overly shy or possibly unintelligent, but that is probably not the case. Her preference to be alone is not related to her abilities. In fact, she may be highly intelligent, needing direction from others to move into areas to use or expand her ideas but also needing private time and space to do so.

As a professional, Dorothy might gravitate to media or technology, areas where she would be able to direct learning without continual and active involvement. She would provide basic information for others to get started on a task.

She expects her co-workers to be able to work independently with minimal direction or instructions. She is likely to work better with experienced staff, who do not need a lot of contact.

She prefers quiet work, without disturbing others. Those who are more outgoing will challenge Dorothy's patience and energy. She would likely exclude those who cannot or will not interact quietly (and minimally).

She needs *solitude.* That is, she needs time and space to be alone. She can move into other "frames of preference," but the amount of energy she has to interact with others will depend on the amount of alone time she has had.

She would prefer to be directed to take on an assignment or do a task. She will do likewise for those she may supervise.

She finds her direction to act from others. She is very good with her hands and is likely to gravitate toward tactile tasks.

She approaches her job with a sense of wanting to do well what she is directed to do. She would probably not initiate new projects but would participate as part of a team on the periphery of action.

She would be an excellent sorter of ideas and might even share some of her thinking (when directed to do so). Her ability to reflect on things would give the group a stable and considered perspective.

She dresses without much consideration of style and in an unfussy way. She wears her hair simply and may not use much, if any, makeup. When the gray began to show, she did not obscure it.

Some might describe her as *plain*, but she would probably not take offense at the description and might even agree with it. On formal occasions, she would dress appropriately but not overdo her appearance. However, she would prefer to avoid crowds and loud celebrations.

Dorothy will not seek actively recognition for her work or accolades for a job done well. As an administrator or supervisor, she is unlikely to do much in the way of acknowledging or rewarding good performance, but she is likely to be aware of problems that may occur. She will intercede only when absolutely necessary.

(Dorothy is not likely to seek an administrative position on her own, but she might be drafted or recruited. A *status quo* organization that does not need much direction or leadership would work best for her. One that required a great deal of interaction would be distressful for her, and she would probably leave after a short period of time. She would more likely be a follower and a good team member. Her Blake-Mouton [1985] style is likely to be more in the direction of production than people.)

Dorothy's preferred administrative style is *autocratic*—assigning tasks and duties. She will direct others to action but will not micromanage or supervise too closely.

She will look to others to generate new ideas and will provide her feedback if she is responsible for the overall running of a program or project. Maintaining the *status quo* with established routines and procedures is her preference. It involves a minimum of interaction and planning.

Dorothy prefers to be *directive*. She will seek information straightforwardly in interchanges with others. She will also respond directly when asked for information—without embellishment, rationalization, or emotion.

If Dorothy has a life issue to resolve, it is likely to be *autonomy*. She may experience long-term intense distress with a focus on what might happen if she is not strong—"Things and people can make me feel bad. Therefore, I will be strong and withdraw, and as I become passive, I can avoid making my own decisions" (Kahler, 1996).

If she does not get her *solitude* needs met positively, she will retreat to a *be-strong* driver position—protecting herself by "cocooning," or spreading herself too thinly. She will use the passive voice more than usual—"It occurred to me . . ."

If Dorothy's distress continues, she will withdraw. The warning signals are either her waiting passively or starting a number of things without finishing them.

This distress may carry over to her personal life. She may become more and more distant (even from those significant other people in her life), or appear embarrassed or shier than usual.

She will wait passively to be directed by others—people or situations. When she is in distress, Dorothy's life is one of increased inaction.

Her preeminent need for solitude overrides any interaction. The more others try to involve her in group activities or projects, the more she is likely to withdraw.

If Dorothy works with a supervisor whose preferences are different from hers or who is intolerant to hers, she is likely to appear disinterested in her job or uncommitted to the mission of the organization. The Thinkers and Persisters with whom she works may distance themselves from her because of her inaction, or they may become critical about her lack of initiative and commitment. The Harmonizers will *sense* her distress and try to help or "fix" her. Neither the criticism nor overattention will be as useful as her finding the solitude she needs.

Dorothy's Profile	
Character Strengths:	Imaginative, reflective, calm
Perceptual Preference:	Inactions (reflections)
Motivational Need:	Solitude
Administrative Style:	Autocratic
Channel:	Directive
Driver:	Be strong
Failure Mechanism:	Withdraws
Life Issue:	Autonomy

(Adapted with permission from Kahler, T. [1996].)

PROBLEM SITUATION

Dorothy, your data archivist, seems to be more withdrawn than usual. She has started several projects—putting her catalog online, re-inventorying the electronic equipment, and reviewing catalogs for new professional development videos—but has finished none of these projects, all of which have been suggested or requested by you. Your annual corporate open house is underway, with staff needing direction from her and a constant flow of traffic through her normally quiet environment.

Symptoms for Consideration

Dorothy is demonstrating that she is not getting the Imaginer *solitude* she needs. Too frequent interaction with others has put this data archivist into distress—people wanting to know where to go, staff asking questions about where to find materials, potential customers wandering through her normally low-traffic area, et cetera.

Suggestions for Action

- Give her a day off—report it as either sick ("mental health") or personal (with her permission) leave. Doing this on a Monday or Friday would be best, since she would be away for at least three days.
- Assign her a reliable staff member to oversee the open house, so she would not have to interact with those who are participating—either staff or visitors.
- Tell her you are thinking about a research service component for the company and want to involve interns as research methodology resource people. Tell her to prepare a plan to expand this idea so you can see how she envisions such a project. You want to review the plan with the pros and

cons, and her oversight before you and she discuss whether it is feasible to implement.
- If she does not already have a private office with a door she can close, provide her with one. If she does, arrange to have one-way glass installed so she can see out but others cannot see into her office.

(Adapted with permission from Kahler, T. [1982].)

REFERENCES

Blake, R. R., & Mouton, J. S. (1985). *The Managerial Grid III: A new look at the classic that has boosted productivity and profits for thousands of corporations worldwide.* Houston, TX: Gulf Publishing Co.

Kahler, T. (1982). *Personality Pattern Inventory studies.* Little Rock, AR: Kahler Communications, Inc.

Kahler, T. (1996). *The advanced Process Communication seminar.* Little Rock, AR: Kahler Communications, Inc.

Chapter Nine

Pure Rebel: Angie

Angie is a *spontaneous, playful,* and *creative* person. (Her given name is Angela Marie, but only her mother calls her that.) She decided to become a graphics designer because she liked the idea and thought it would be fun. Her life focuses outwardly. She prefers to react to things and issues, knowing quickly what she likes and what she does not. Her home is exciting but may appear chaotic to those who see the world through more orderly lenses. The rooms are bright and stimulating.

Angie experiences the world through her likes and dislikes (reactions). She prefers to be around others who will stimulate her and to work in an exciting environment—both physically and intellectually. She is very good at coming up with very creative—some might say, "bizarre"—approaches to situations. Routines bore her. She prefers to work on projects that are exciting—if they are also fun, even better. When she is asked a question or for information, she tends to react spontaneously—sometimes without thinking through the issue.

She prefers to be around others with high energy. When working with staff, she will assign them work mostly according to the program, but will embellish the presentation in a fun way if she can. She may facilitate a discussion of issues but is likely to encourage creative thinking—sometimes, the more outlandish, the better. Her preference to interact in fun ways may give others (usually Thinkers and Persisters) the impression she is not focused or dedicated to the venture, but her approach is definitely in the minority. Her preference for contact and in a stimulating environment is related to her ability to "color outside the lines." In fact, she may be highly intelligent, sometimes needing the freedom to tap into her store of creativity.

Angie gravitates to art, music, or drama—areas where she would be able to emote and to stimulate others to do likewise. She provides basic information for staff to get started on a task, but she is likely to expect them to think divergently some of the time.

She expects staff to be able to interact with others and devise projects that involve a group of colleagues. She is likely to work better with those who prefer a lot of contact and who are willing to look at things differently. Staff who require structure and direction will have difficulty with Angie's style. In fact, they may find her energy tiresome . . . and tiring. Similarly, Angie may become frustrated—even sarcastic—with those who are reluctant to explore their creative side.

Her approach is to joke and, possibly, tease good-naturedly first. Those who are more outgoing will appeal to Angie, but they may also distract and redirect the project. Her work area is likely to be noisy and busy. The project structure and rules are probably few and typically unenforced.

Serious disrupters of activities are difficult for Angie to redirect. She is more likely to argue with them. She needs assistance with those who want to bring structure and order to a project. She *blames* them for criticizing, even though they might be responding to her style or environment.

She needs *contact*. That is, she needs to be around people and situations that are exciting and stimulating. She can move into other "frames of preference," but the amount of energy she has to interact with others will depend on the amount of fun time she has had. She prefers to be delegated an assignment or do a task; she will do likewise for those she supervises.

This delegation would be interpreted as, "do it the way *you* want. It's your project." However, if a project delegated to her is accompanied by structure or specific parameters, they may get in the way of Angie's approach or creativity.

She finds her motivation to act from other people and things. She is very good with her hands and is probably very coordinated, especially with fine-motor tasks.

She approaches her job with a sense of excitement and challenge. She will probably initiate new projects that allow her to flex her creativity.

She would participate as part of a team of her buddies. She would be an excellent generator of ideas—especially highly creative ones. Her ability to react to things might be difficult for the rest of the group, especially those who need and want structure and logical thinking—but they would not usually be within her circle of colleagues.

Angie is very good in brainstorming situations. She is someone who searches for alternatives, going beyond the known and the obvious and the satisfactory.

Pure Rebel: Angie

She prefers movement into new, uncharted territory instead of judgment, tradition, and clarity. Angie has a strong ability to think *laterally*—cutting across established patterns to generate new concepts and perceptions.

She dresses without consideration of style or the organization. She is likely to attract attention with her nonconformity.

She might appear rumpled or unkempt—or unironed. Her clothes are likely to be bright—and maybe uncoordinated. The colors she chooses may be loud—especially her hair and nail polish.

Responses from those who think/believe there is/ought to be a dress code might be, "How can she dress like that? Doesn't she know how important appearance and image are in business?" If she does dress up or dress down, she would be playing a role. If it is fun for her, she will do it.

Angie does not actively seek recognition for her work or accolades for a job done well. As an administrator or supervisor, she is likely to give "high fives" as a way of acknowledging or rewarding good performance, but she would have to move to another part of her personality to offer more traditional recognition—letters, certificates, plaques, etc.

Angie's preferred administrative style is *laissez-faire*. She will delegate tasks to others but will not micromanage or supervise too closely.

She will look to others to generate new ideas and will interact with them if they ask for her involvement and feedback. Maintaining the *status quo* with established routines and procedures bores her. She prefers to test new areas of solution. She is stymied often in traditional organizations and will leave a dull situation in favor of someplace more exciting.

(Since Angie operates freely, she is like to be focused externally—outside of traditional "lines." Her Blake-Mouton [1985] orientation would be toward the *1, 1* position of being disengaged. This does not reflect a lack of commitment to the organization, only to supervise from a distance.)

Angie is *emotive*. She interacts energetically with others. When asked for information, she responds playfully, but will eventually get to the point—especially if others seem exasperated with her less-than-direct attitude.

If Angie has a life issue to resolve, it is likely to be *responsibility*. She may experience long-term intense distress with a focus on what might happen if she does not try hard to understand—"If you don't do the thinking for me, then I won't be happy. Therefore, I will try hard. When you don't make me feel good by thinking for me, then it's your fault I feel bad, and as long as I blame you, I can avoid the responsibility of feeling good with self-love" (Kahler, 1996).

If she does not get her *contact* needs met positively, she will retreat to a *"try hard"* driver position—feigning confusion and inviting others to think for her: *"I don't get it."* She will invite "games" more than usual—"Yes . . . but" is one of her favorites. (You offer her a solution that she seems to accept, but then invites you to offer another possibility or defend your idea: "Yes, I heard what you said, but . . .") If Angie's distress continues, she will go to a position of "I'm OK; you're not." The warning signals are her becoming negative and complaining, blameless, or blameful.

This distress may carry over to her personal life. She may become more and more irresponsible, and blame others when things go awry. She expects others to make things right—". . . after all, it was their *fault* in the first place." When she is in distress, Angie's life is one of blaming.

Her preeminent need for contact takes on a negative air. The more others try to rationalize and be logical, the more she is likely to blame: *"See what you made me do."*

If Angie works with a supervisor whose preferences are different from hers or who is intolerant to hers, she is likely to sabotage her job or a project as a way of getting the contact she needs—even if it is negative. The Thinkers and Persisters with whom she works may find her "irresponsible" behavior to be exasperating or frustrating, and they will become critical about her lack of commitment and obeying the rules. The Harmonizers will *sense* her distress and try to help or fix her. Neither the criticism nor overattention will be as useful as her finding the contact she needs.

Angie's Profile	
Character Strengths:	Spontaneous, creative, playful
Perceptual Preference:	Reactions (likes and dislikes)
Motivational Need:	Contact (playful)
Administrative Style:	Laissez-faire
Channel:	Emotive
Driver:	Try hard
Failure Mechanism:	Blames
Life Issue:	Responsibility

(Adapted with permission from Kahler, T. [1996].)

PROBLEM SITUATION

Angie, your graphics designer, is consistently late with reports; she even turns them in occasionally using an artist's drawing pencil—smudged and illegible. She is not supervising the comings and goings of staff carefully. Recently, there was a loud argument between two of her staff. Two others farther away had to intervene. When you, as her supervisor, asked her why she did not attend to the situation, her response was, "Oh, I didn't realize they needed my help."

Symptoms for Consideration

By acting irresponsibly, Angie is giving you definite clues that her Rebel needs of playful *contact* are not being met. She may be too mired in routine—filling out reports, providing a structured environment for her staff, etc. She is not having the energizing fun she needs to charge her batteries.

Suggestions for Action

- Make contact with Angie at the next opportunity with some high energy—"Cool outfit!" "Wow! I didn't know you could walk by putting one foot in front of the other." (Be careful that the message or the tone is not teasing or sarcastic but more of a playful observation. You may see the jargon and playfulness as silly, but Angie will like this type of *contact*.)
- Ask her to redecorate some aspect of the building in need of a new look, and give her free rein to do it. (If you are afraid of something too bizarre, provide some gentle but not-too-restrictive parameters.)
- Ask her to serve as a resource person or advisor to any activity or productions requiring a creative approach. Do not assign her these tasks, but give her the option of participating when she can contribute and *enjoy* herself.
- If you need help with a very kinesthetic program (e.g., office party), be sure she is on the committee or ask her to participate in helping to be sure everyone has a good time.

(Adapted with permission from Kahler, T. [1996].)

REFERENCES

Blake, R. R., & Mouton, J. S. (1985). *The Managerial Grid III: A new look at the classic that has boosted productivity and profits for thousands of corporations worldwide.* Houston, TX: Gulf Publishing Co.

Kahler, T. (1982). *Personality Pattern Inventory studies.* Little Rock, AR: Kahler Communications, Inc.

Kahler, T. (1996). *The advanced Process Communication seminar.* Little Rock, AR: Kahler Communications, Inc.

Chapter Ten

Pure Promoter: Doug

(Note: Only about 5% of the North American population has a Promoter base. Those in Promoter Phase are also a small percentage.)

Doug is an *adaptable, persuasive,* and *charming* person. (His given name is "Robert Douglas," but he likes to be called "Doug.") He prefers to work in an active and stimulating environment. His life focuses outwardly. He wants action and quick payoffs—getting to the "bottom line" and completing projects. His home reflects the outward trappings of an active lifestyle. The rooms are colorful and filled with trophies—stuffed animals from hunting, expensive furniture, exercise equipment, and possibly trendy artwork.

Doug experiences the world through actions. He prefers to get into projects that will be completed in short order, and to work in an environment where rewards are quick in coming. He is very good at cutting through *red tape* and finding fast routes to intermediate goals.

Routines bore him. He prefers to work on projects that lead to tangible rewards. If they are also interesting, that is OK but not necessary.

When he is asked a question or for information, he tends to respond directly. He is not likely to explain or rationalize things unless someone else pursues an issue or topic. He will talk in jargon and action words and will use nicknames or pseudo-endearments when addressing others: "Hey, babe [which might be interpreted as sexist, but he might use it with men, too]. Let's get this show going. We've got to get things done."

He prefers to be around others who prefer short-term attainment. When working with staff, he will assign them work that can be completed quickly, but will not spend a lot of time providing extensive feedback or much rationale of the importance of the work.

Format and details are not as important as the overall assignment. He may plan a discussion of issues but is likely to encourage moving to resolution quickly.

His preference for the "bottom line" may give others the impression he is not committed or dedicated to the organizational venture—that impression may be accurate to some degree. His preference for action and short-term outcomes is related to his ability to get things done. He may be highly intelligent, but his lack of attention to detail many times may lead others to assume he is not dependable and focused only on what he can get out of a project.

Doug gravitates to areas where he can be active. He provides basic information to get started on a task, but he is unlikely to demonstrate skills for others to model.

He interacts with others in persuasive and charming ways, especially if they accomplish objectives more quickly. He is likely to work better with others who are oriented kinesthetically. People tend to like him.

Individuals who require structure and direction will have difficulty with Doug's style. In fact, they may find his "bottom-line" preference ill placed and confusing. Similarly, Doug may become frustrated—even cynical—with those who persevere with their work—that is, those who take whatever time they need or who are not satisfied quickly.

His approach to lengthy projects would be to manipulate compliance and redirection first. Those who are canny and smooth in extricating themselves from trouble will appeal to Doug.

His work area is busy and outcome-oriented. Serious disrupters of activities meet with vindictiveness. He sets them up to fail or be excluded.

He does not have time for those who dawdle. He also places the "blame" on them for slowing things down, even though they might be responding to his style or environment—or to a situation he had orchestrated.

Doug needs *incidence.* That is, he needs many opportunities for action and payoffs. He can move into other "frames of preference," but the amount of energy he has to interact with others will depend on the number of things he has accomplished and the wealth (tangible or psychological) he has accumulated from them.

He prefers to be directed to an assignment or do a task. He will do likewise for those he supervises. However, he may move ahead with decisions without consulting others.

A typical approach he sees as positive because it gets things done is, "Do what is necessary and apologize for it later." As as administrator, he is not likely to be questioned for his decision making, unless the outcomes are less-than-salutary for the organization.

His subordinates would find most of his decisions falling into Barnard's (1938) "zone of indifference"—that is, there might not be a strong commitment to the decision, but it would be carried out nevertheless. His parental style will disenfranchise others in the organization, and his "My-way-or-the-highway" attitude will leave him with few close colleagues. However, his easy way with people will make him attractive, until he gets into trouble for not following through with plans or programs.

He finds his motivation to act from others. He approaches his job with a sense of challenge and seeks tangible accomplishments. He focuses on perfecting behaviors that will bring him the payoffs he seeks.

He will participate as part of a team of his "buddies," especially if they are mutually outcome-oriented. He is not likely to generate new ideas, unless they will help him accomplish things more quickly.

His preference for the "bottom line" might be difficult for the rest of the group, especially those who need and want structure and logical thinking—but they are not likely to be within his circle of associates. Doug is very good in finding the quickest way to get a project finished, but he might overlook some of the details in getting there.

He needs the assistance of Angie to generate creative solutions, Dorothy to carry out the mundane operations, and Alfred or Matthew to attend to the details. Without their assistance, he flounders and, possibly, fails.

He dresses flamboyantly. He will attract attention with his flaunting style. He might have bold jewelry. His clothes are likely to be trendy. The colors he chooses would be reds and blacks.

Others (again, usually the Thinkers and Persisters) in the organization see his style as inappropriate. They might suggest he tone down his appearance, if they were directed by him to "Tell me how I look." He would not change and would discount or disregard negative responses.

Doug actively seeks rewards for his work or tangible acknowledgment for a job done well. As an administrator or supervisor, he provides incentives as a way of stimulating productivity. He will give monetary rewards if he has discretionary monies available, or looks for benefactors outside of the organization.

Doug's preferred administrative style is *autocratic*. He delegates the detail work to others but does not micromanage or supervise too closely.

Maintaining the *status quo* with routines and procedures bores him, unless there is a consistent pattern of rewards and payoffs connected with established practice. He prefers to pursue a new route or create new alliances to move toward organizational productivity. (He, like Dorothy, prefers more of a task orientation.)

He is stymied often in traditional organizations and flits from one to another in search of tangible rewards. Since he prefers action, he is seen as a *change agent*. Because change is highly uncomfortable, especially in stable organizations, Doug is frustrated quickly if he does not effect change—and he moves on.

Doug prefers to be *directive*. When he is energized and OK, he interacts straightforwardly in interchanges with others. When asked for information, he responds directly, without embellishment or the need to explain. However, he might try to manipulate a situation that was is "going his way," even being seductive in the attempt.

If Doug has a life issue to resolve, it is likely to be *bonding*. He may experience long-term intense distress with a focus on what might happen if others are not strong—"Things and people can make you feel bad. Therefore, you will have to be strong and abandon anyone who gets too close. As long as I abandon you, I can avoid bonding with you" (Kahler, 1996).

If he does not get his *incidence* needs met positively, he will retreat to a *"You have to be strong"* driver position—being unsupportive and expecting others to fend for themselves. If Doug's distress continues, he will *blame* and go to a position of "I'm OK; you're not." He will set up negative drama—attempting to get others into arguments or disagreements as a way of achieving the incidence he needs.

The warning signals are his ignoring or breaking rules or trying to get them changed for himself only. He will say "You . . ." when talking about himself—*"Ya know when you're driving down the highway and going fast, ya have to look out for the 'fuzz'."* (Meaning: "When I am driving down the highway too fast, I have to watch for radar or police." But then he probably has a radar detector as one of his car toys.)

This distress may carry over to his personal life. He may become more and more manipulative and take high risks. He may use alcohol and drugs to excess. He might be seductive to achieve an end. He will expect others to "take it." When they do not, his response would be "Ah hah! I knew they weren't strong enough."

When he is in distress, Doug blames. His preeminent need for incidence takes on a negative air. The more others try to redirect him, the more manipulative and defensive he is likely to be.

If Doug works with someone whose preferences are different from his or who is intolerant to his, he is likely to create some negative drama—getting others to argue and become competitive with each other. The Thinkers and Persisters with whom he works find his manipulative behavior unacceptable, and they avoid him and distance themselves from him if possible. The Harmonizers will try to help him, but they are likely to be seduced and hurt. Neither the criticism nor overadaptation will work. Doug will become productive only if he finds incidence in his professional and personal life.

Pure Promoter: Doug

Doug's Profile	
Character Strengths:	Adaptable, persuasive, charming
Perceptual Preference:	Actions
Motivational Need:	Incidence
Administrative Style:	Autocratic
Channel:	Directive
Driver:	You must be strong
Failure Mechanism:	Manipulates
Life Issue:	Bonding

(Adapted with permission from Kahler, T. [1996].)

PROBLEM SITUATION

Doug is new to your staff, with five years of previous experience. It is a very rainy day, and you notice that your new staff member, Doug, is parking in the space designated clearly, "Employee of the Month." This is a prominent space, close to the building entrance and reserved for another staff member, who earned this.

Symptoms for Consideration

Doug obviously is not respecting the reserved parking space or the reason it was reserved in the first place. He has broken the rules, manipulated the situation to suit himself. His actions may precipitate a confrontation—between him and the "Employee of the Month," with you as possible referee (negative drama).

He is demonstrating Promoter distress of not getting his *incidence* needs met through his manipulation and expects others to *be strong* as a way of coping and accommodating. He is likely to attempt to be charming and possibly seductive when he is approached, and will probably downplay the importance of this breach of etiquette or protocol with, "It was raining real hard and I thought you wouldn't mind if I *borrowed* your space."

He might also attempt to pacify his colleague with promise of a future reward, which is unlikely ever to be proffered. (Note: You are unlikely to encounter few people in Promoter phase and fewer with a Promoter base.)

Suggestions for Action

- Do a "one-minute reprimand," (à la Blanchard & Johnson, 1982): "That space is reserved for the 'Employee of the Month.' Don't park there again until you have attained the honor." Do not preach or explain the importance of the award. (Document the action in a "memorandum of understanding"

to emphasize your point, thanking Doug for his cooperation. Note also that you will have to be direct with Doug. He will not perceive your directness as being rude; however, being direct [using an *autocratic* style] may not be the way you usually handle situations. In this case, you will connect with Doug and invite him to change more effectively than any of the other interaction styles.)
- Invite Doug to submit a plan for competition for other parking spaces to be reserved or other "perks" for performance.

(Adapted with permission from Kahler, T. [1996].)

REFERENCES

Barnard, C. I. (1938). *The functions of the executive.* Cambridge, MA: Harvard University Press.

Blanchard, K. H., & Johnson, S. (1982). *The one minute manager.* New York, NY: Berkley Books.

Kahler, T. (1996). *The advanced Process Communication seminar.* Little Rock, AR: Kahler Communications, Inc.

Section III

PUTTING THINGS TOGETHER: BUILDING EFFECTIVE COMMUNICATION SKILLS

Chapter Eleven

Dealing with Conflict

Many successful builders have their special tools and techniques. It may be a favorite hammer, or a specific location on a job site to start laying brick, or a way to finish a joint.

Effective leaders have their favorite "tools," too. In most cases, these leaders prefer to stick to the tools or methods that have worked in the past—this is a useful way to address situations that are similar to others they have faced before.

The problem is that the favorite "hammer" may not work well all of the time. It may be too heavy for some finishing work or too cumbersome for a delicate job. A lighter "tool" might be better—and more effective.

PREPARATION

Administrators prepare for their jobs in two ways—formally and informally. The formal preparation comes through course work at colleges and universities, and through other organized activities, such as workshops and readings. Informal preparation comes through life and professional experience.

We take what we have learned and apply it in situations that seem appropriate, or we observe others doing things effectively and try to emulate their methods. But not all situations can be resolved using the same approach, even if it has worked before. When we use an approach that does not work, then we try it again, find a different approach, ask or tell someone else to do *it*, ignore the situation, or give up.

Of course, repeating an approach that has not worked is usually met with similar results. Finding a different way to resolve a conflict is useful but may be time-consuming. Giving in to someone else or ignoring the circumstances removes the situation from our immediate concern. Giving up does little more than put the situation aside without resolution.

In more formal terms, there are a number of techniques to manage conflict: *avoidance, suppression, domination, compromise,* and *integration* (or problem solving). The behaviors and their rubrics are listed below.

Conflict Management Style	Behaviors
Avoidance	Giving up/withdrawing
Suppression	Ignoring/denying/smoothing
Domination	Telling
Compromise	Finding alternatives
Integration	Finding creative alternatives

By using the first four techniques, the administrator does little more than manage the situation. If there is conflict, it is set aside—for a time. Using *integration*—the conflict management style that seeks creative alternatives—is the only true way to *resolve* conflict. The leader who adopts this style has a high degree of concern for both people and production (Blake & Mouton, 1985) and uses a team approach to problem solving.

MANAGING CONFLICT

What Is Conflict?

Conflict occurs when people interacting with each other *perceive* their goals to be incompatible. Here, perception is reality.

Whether or not the goals are truly incompatible is overshadowed by how people see the situation—each through his or her own screens. (This is akin to the communication screens shown in the Communication Rainbow in Chapter 3.) When we bring different perceptions to a conflict, we may have difficulty empathizing or seeing things through someone else's lenses.

Conflict arises for various reasons:

- Ambiguous roles
- Conflicting interests
- Communication barriers
- Dependence of one party (on another)
- Differentiation of organization (causing confusion or imbalance of authority)
- Need for consensus

- Behavior regulations or rules
- Unresolved prior conflicts (Maurer, 1991, pp. 3–4)

Moreover, if we perceive we have incompatible goals, we may want to *win*: win our position, win the day, or simply get what we want, regardless of the needs of others. Conflict does not go away without the parties agreeing that it is gone. It is gone only when the situation turns into *win-win*.

What May Not Be Effective

In attempting to resolve conflict if there is an element of losing, then the conflict is not resolved. Different types of people need to be approached differently when they are in conflict.

Their personality types will describe patterns that may help them get what they need, possibly overriding the situation. That is, their needs will overshadow the situation—shifting the focus to themselves and away from the problem. The likelihood is that they are in distress and will show the predictable patterns described for the six people you have just met.

Another way to look at unresolved conflict is to consider that the participants are not getting their needs met. This is the *distress* (or miscommunication) component of the Process Communication Model (Kahler, 1982). The first degree is the *driver* behavior we may see many times during a day. It is mild and indicates the beginning of distress.

If the lack of need fulfillment continues and gets more pronounced, we may see a second degree of distress. Someone in the interaction will be seen as "not OK," and a particular conflict management style will emerge.

Avoidance takes Harmonizers and Imaginers out of the situation or puts the situation aside. The conflict is not resolved; they just are not a part of it anymore: "I am not going to deal with this," Imaginer Dorothy might say as she withdraws in an attempt to get her need for *solitude* met.

Barbara (the Harmonizer) will be distressed at the conflict, especially if she is involved directly. She either will attempt to appease ("I just want everyone to be happy") or overadapt ("How can I make this better for you?"), trying to find acceptance of herself as a person.

> Barbara (Harmonizer): "Dorothy, would it be possible to postpone putting the professional resources on computer . . . for a while? It's probably my fault that we are moving ahead, but I am uncomfortable with the confusion it may bring to the staff."
>
> Dorothy (Imaginer): (Silence)

Barbara: "I know we talked about this and I really appreciate all you have done... Oh my! Things are in such a mess. Would it be OK if we talked more later?"

Dorothy: "OK!"

Suppression denies the conflict exists: "You really don't hate your sister," Barbara would offer, trying to bring harmony into family chaos. (She sees the staff in her organization as extended family.) Angie, the Rebel, might look for ways to get her playful contact need met by ignoring the conflict: "Oh, yeah! Well, we can't deal with that now. We have other fish to fry."

Barbara (Harmonizer): "I hate to interrupt. I know you are planning for your new project. I am a bit uneasy about the blank space, so I am wondering how will you design the walls? I know it's a bother, but I need to order the paint."

Angie (Rebel): "Yeah, I know I did promise, but I have a super idea. How about giving the custodial staff the paint and letting them come up with their own design?"

Barbara: "Oh, I don't know. I am not sure if that would work—giving them free rein like that. I mean, you are so creative and everything . . ."

Angie: "Aw, c'mon. It'll be fun—and the custodians can be as creative as they want."

An individual who relies on *domination* to manage conflict attempts to control behavior by dictating the approach to resolve (not really) the conflict in which one party wholly *wins* and the other party *loses*.

"Here's what *we*'re going to do . . ." action-oriented Doug would assert, trying to cut through any protracted discussion and get to the "bottom line." Someone in a position of power (or perceived power) and who is willing to use that power to get what she or he wants uses this technique. The other party is given little choice but to follow the dictum.

(This will work in many situations unless the order falls into the *zone of non-compliance* [Barnard, 1938]. Non-compliance may be tantamount to subversion or insubordination. At times, orders clash sharply with the personal values of people, and they cannot obey.)

Doug (Promoter): "Ya know. Let's just scrap the policy manual and start over."

Matthew (Persister): "What?! Do you mean to tell me you want to throw away all of what we've been doing all these years?"

Doug: "Yeah! That stuff's not working anyway. Ya know when you're looking for an answer, ya rarely find it in that policy manual. Ya gotta go where the action is."

Matthew: "I am not sure this is the way to proceed. Specifically, what you are proposing?"

Doug: "We're gonna start from scratch, and too bad for anyone who doesn't like it."

Compromise is characterized by each party giving up something in order to reach a decision or to move on: "I'll meet you halfway." Alfred, our Thinker, and Matthew, our Persister, will approach the issue of incompatible goals rationally and try to reason through the situation.

This will address the recognition of their work they both need: "If the conflict is resolved, you will see me in a good light." Alfred's *good* work is recognized; Matthew's contribution to organizational goals will be seen as important. As a result of the agreement, Alfred will be able to move on to the other things in his full schedule (time structure), and Matthew will have some of his conviction need met.

While this does allow the issue to be put aside, the goals that led to the conflict still may be incompatible. Since neither party was fully satisfied, the conflict—the incompatible goals—may resurface if the individuals have an ongoing relationship.

Union negotiations provide a good example of this. It is highly unlikely that unions get all they want for their members in a bargaining agreement. They typically ask for more than they know they will get, and organizations usually offer less than they know they will have to give.

This pattern underpins the unwritten bargaining rules. As a result, the incompatible goals likely will arise when the next contract negotiation surfaces. In this example of *interdependence,* the conflicting parties depend on each other because they often work together.

(I remember how perplexed a colleague of mine was when he followed the rules in what appeared to be a negotiation. He asked for a certain position, and the other party thought it was reasonable. His response was, "I should have asked for more," even though he got what he wanted.)

Alfred (Thinker): "We need to resolve the situation about health care."

Matthew (Persister): "I don't believe this community is ready for our interference in family matters."

Alfred: "How about if I come up with a plan that I think the community will accept?"

Matthew: "If you mean working on this by yourself, what exactly is your plan? Will you pass it by me first? I would like a chance to review it."

These are all techniques used by administrators. More effective leaders look for more lasting resolution.

RESOLVING CONFLICT INTEGRATIVELY

The first four techniques of managing conflict truly do not resolve the situation. Instead, they may allow us to put the situation aside for the time being. The true *win-win* outcome can only be reached integratively.

In resolution through *integration*, both parties contribute and neither party gives up anything to arrive at a result. One of the earliest proponents of this strategy was Mary Parker Follett. She saw true resolution of conflict to be achieved through cooperation, collaboration, and collegiality. "Integration involves invention, and the clever thing is to recognize this, and not to let one's thinking stay within the boundaries of two alternatives which are mutually exclusive" (Follett in Metcalf & Urwick, 1940, p. 33).

Empowerment is the key to using integration effectively. It is the use of power *with* colleagues, co-workers and subordinates rather than power *over* them.

Many experts in the field of organizational theory have explored the notion of power in organizations. One of the most famous views of power comes from Max Weber (1947). He saw power as being both positional and attributional—related to who we are in the organization or who we are as people. When power is abused or misused in interactions, people may assume positions of dominance or submission.

From a Transactional Analysis (the basis of Process Communication) perspective, these positions are either "I'm OK; you're not OK" (dominance), or "I'm not OK; you're OK" (submission). If "I'm OK" and you're not, I am assuming the role of a *persecutor* looking for a *victim* (Karpman, 1968). These roles emerge during the distress described by Process Communication when the needs of Thinkers, Persisters, Rebels, and Promoters are not met positively (Kahler, 1978).

If "I'm not OK" and you are, I am a *victim* looking for a *persecutor* (Karpman, 1968). This is the role of Harmonizers and Imaginers in distress (Kahler, 1978). An imbalance of power can magnify distress.

Organizationally, power is the *ability* to act. This is combined with *authority* and *responsibility*—authority being the *right* to act and responsibility being the *obligation* to act (Corwin, 1965). The effective leader shares authority through appropriate delegation, retaining ultimate responsibility. Power, then, describes both the physical, mental, and organizational ability of individuals to do their jobs.

It means sharing to the end of accomplishing a task. To achieve this shared empowerment, it is crucial for the parties to have mutual understanding of the task, the organization, and the goals. The appropriate use of *power, authority,* and *responsibility* may open the door to integration and keep people focused on resolving conflict positively. These are the tools of an effective leader.

POINTS TO PONDER

- Conflict exists in all organization. Effective leaders must find ways to manage conflict, or, even better, to resolve conflict.
- Conflict can serve to divide organization, or it can be used to move organizations ahead.
- Recognizing that conflict is the *perception* of incompatible goals, leaders must seek the win-win position for lasting resolution.
- Integration of ideas and participation by the conflicted parties are the only ways to resolve conflict. All other methods of conflict management either ignore or set aside conflict for a period. The perceived incompatibility does not disappear.

REFERENCES

Barnard, C. I. (1938). *The functions of the executive.* Cambridge, MA: Harvard University Press.

Blake, R. R., & Mouton, J. S. (1985). *The Managerial Grid III: A new look at the classic that has boosted productivity and profits for thousands of corporations worldwide.* Houston, TX: Gulf Publishing Co.

Corwin, R. G. (1965). *A sociology of education: Emerging patterns of class, status, and power in the public schools.* New York, NY: Appleton-Century-Crofts.

Kahler, T. (1978). *T. A. revisited.* Little Rock, AR: Human Development Publications.

Kahler, T. (1982). *The Process Communication management seminar.* Little Rock, AR: Kahler Communications, Inc.

Karpman, S. (1968). Fairy tales and script drama analysis. *Transactional Analysis Bulletin, 7*(26), 39–43.

Maurer, R. E. (1991). *Managing conflict: Tactics for school administrators.* Needham Heights, MA: Allyn & Bacon.

Metcalf, H. C., & Urwick, L. (Eds.). (1940). *Dynamic administration: The collected papers of Mary Parker Follett.* New York, NY: Harper & Row.

Weber, M. (1947). *The theory of social and economic organization* (tr. by A. M. Henderson & T. Parsons). New York, NY: Oxford Univ. Press.

Chapter Twelve

Solving Problems Cooperatively
A Blueprint For Success

Conflict in organizations is inevitable. Resolving conflict and the problems that come from conflict is the true test of the effective leader. Succeeding as a conflict resolver brings into consideration three competencies of leadership:

- *Diagnosing,* the cognitive competency—understanding the situation.
- *Adapting,* the behavioral competency that helps close the gap between where things are and where you want them to be.
- *Communicating,* the process competency that allows others to understand and accept the situation and its need for resolution. (Hersey, Blanchard, & Johnson, 2013)

At times, it may seem the situation cannot be resolved—deciding whether to go to your child's birthday party or attend an important professional conference. If the dates for each are set and overlap, then you may have to choose.

What if another alternative will allow you to do both, but it might mean looking at the situation differently? It is this possibility that may allow you to be integrative—to get what you want without losing and not causing others to lose either.

It may require you to think in a different way, putting aside the structure you have used before, which may have been to choose one event (usually the professional conference). One way to do both of the above would be to go to the professional meeting and celebrate with your child when you return, even though it would be a different kind of celebration. You might also watch a recording of the party and ask your child to describe the events. With current technology, you could have a video chat with your child on the day of the party, using Skype, Face Time, or other software.

We may settle for compromise because each party wins a bit, but each party also loses a bit. "Compromise does not create, it deals with what already exists; integration creates something new" (Follett in Metcalf & Urwick, 1940, p. 35).

In integration, we find stability. The organization or relationship can progress because there is no residue from the conflict. However, we must be willing to be honest and open about the issue.

We must trust and be willing to trust (an important concept in organizational effectiveness; see Ouchi, 1982). "The first rule . . . for obtaining integration is to put your cards on the table, face the real issue, uncover the conflict, bring the whole thing into the open" (Follett in Urwick & Metcalf, 1940, p. 38).

One problem here is that people may not be fully open or forthcoming if they fear that the other party to the conflict might use that information against them. That is, they are afraid to trust the other party because they might lose something—the argument, the issue at hand, the advantage. Withholding information can stymie the use of integration to resolve the conflict.

The differences that produce conflict can disrupt organizations. At the very least, they are distracting, but they can also be divisive. While something productive may arise from resolving conflict, there are some general guidelines to consider:

1. Differences are best resolved by those who differ, not by some third party.
2. The organization can function best when the authority system remains intact.
3. Wherever possible, let both sides win.
4. Memories are fallible; accept that fact.
5. Only the dead keep secrets. (Informal intra-organizational communication networks are usually very healthy.)
6. People hear what they want to hear and report the version they want known.
7. Some differences are irreconcilable. (Glatthorn & Adams, 1983, pp. 59–60)

Within organizations there is an ongoing interdependence, the constant interaction that brings people together on a regular basis. There are few who operate independently. Hence, people work best when their differences are allayed, or when their differences do not interfere with operations, programs, or projects. When differences remain and are a continual source of conflict, more time may be spent on resolving problems than accomplishing the objectives of programs.

DIAGNOSING

What Gets in the Way?

The way we normally think about, feel about, believe about, react to, reflect on, or act on a situation may limit our ability to perceive things differently. The tools we know best provide us with preferred perceptions and interactions. When we *accept* that there are other ways to view things, then we begin the process of understanding multiple possibilities.

The conceptual blocks we may have hinder our perceiving a problem or conceiving its solution effectively. These blocks may be *perceptual* (limits on the way we process information), *emotional* (the fears and reactions that limit our responses), *cultural and environmental* (traditional and accepted patterns of response), and *intellectual and expressive* (lack of correct information or language) (Adams, 2001).

To return to the condominium analogy and the concept of shifting (moving into other frames of preference), we recall the sample personality structure we saw in Chapter 4—the base Thinker in a Persister phase (perhaps, this is Alfred). When we examine the graphic (below), we also note some other things.

While Alfred is motivated currently by recognition of his work as being important and valuable and for his conviction, we also see that he has *staged* (completed a phase) through his Harmonizer. This means he has strength in accessing his emotions and can be sensitive to the feelings of others.

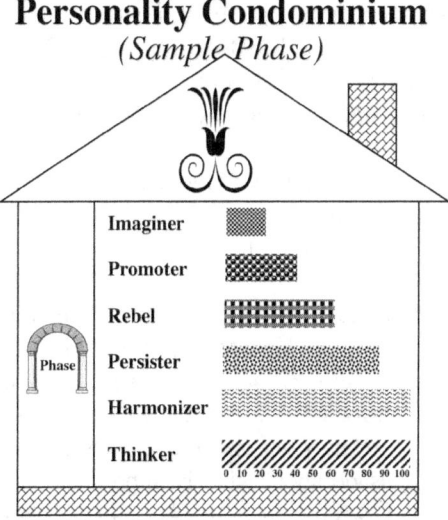

Figure 12.1. Sample Phase. *Source*: Kahler Communications Inc.

We also see something else. The floors above the Persister phase are less full, less "furnished." The amount of relative energy Alfred has is substantially less with each higher floor.

When we access the preferences of another person and his or her personality type, we go to that floor in our structure. So when I want to be playful, I go to my Rebel floor. I get there by way of an elevator.

Alfred has about 60% Rebel energy—his Rebel floor is about 60% furnished, a fair amount. If he has reason to tap into his Rebel, he will find sufficient tools to interact with someone needing *playful contact*.

The reason he might *choose* to go there is because someone or something in his environment has invited him to do so. His son may want to play with him, or he may be asked to find a creative approach to a problem at work, or Angie may *need* him to allow her to approach a situation creatively.

Of course, as with any invitation, we can accept or reject it. If Alfred chooses to accept the invitation, he will have to *call* his elevator to get him there.

His ability to call the elevator depends on whether he is in distress or not. If Alfred (a base Thinker) is sufficiently motivated through recognition of his work and acceptance of his conviction (his Persister phase needs), he can push the call button, get on his elevator, and go to his Rebel floor.

Recalling the preferences from Chapter 4: When we have the need or desire to access different parts of who we are, we go to that floor of our personality.

- When I want to be logical, I go to my Thinker floor.
- When I want to be sensitive, I go to my Harmonizer floor.
- When I want to be dedicated, I go to my Persister floor.
- When I want to be reflective, I go to my Imaginer floor.
- When I want to be playful, I go to my Rebel floor.
- When I want to be adaptable, I go to my Promoter floor.

If Alfred's needs are not met, he will move through the predictable patterns of negative attempts to get the same needs met. He will not have the inclination (or energy) to push the call button and will not go to his Rebel floor. He will reject the invitation.

In this distress, we will see him interacting first with either the actual or virtual finger pointing of the "You have to be perfect to be OK" driver: *"You got a 96 on that test. What exactly, precisely, happened to the other four points?"* He will be hypercritical, focusing on what is wrong rather than what is right.

Continuing failure to get his needs met might bring out an *attack*. Alfred may become preachy, or crusade about what is important, with the overtone that anyone who disagrees is wrong: *"You need to understand how important it is that you excel. Preparing well for the future is critical to your success in life."*

Solving Problems Cooperatively

The end result is that he will not access his Rebel. He will reject the invitation from his son to play, thereby setting up possible distress for his son, whose (playful) contact need will not be met with his father.

As we look further at the condominium, we note that Alfred's Promoter and Imaginer floors are very sparsely furnished. Interacting with Promoters or Imaginers from *their* perspective and through *their* preferences will be somewhat difficult for him. He may access his Promoter or Imaginer, but he will not do so for long because of limited energy.

As Alfred runs out of energy, he will invite others to get in their elevators and move to a floor where he has more energy, such as his Persister. If the other person has sufficient Persister energy, a productive interaction is likely. However, if the other person has as little Persister energy as Alfred has Imaginer energy, then a meeting that focuses on values and opinions is not going to last long. Table 12.1 shows what may happen in dealing with conflict when we are *stuck*.

Table 12.1. Distress Patterns, Conflict Style, & Masks (© Kahler Communications, Inc.)

Personality	First Degree	Second Degree	Conflict Mgt.	Mask
Harmonizer	Overadapts	Invites criticism	Avoidance; Suppression	Drooper (I'm not OK)
Thinker	Does not delegate	Overcontrols	Domination; Compromise	Attacker (You're not OK)
Persister	Focuses negatively	Pushes beliefs	Domination; Compromise	Attacker (You're not OK)
Imaginer	Does not finalize	Withdraws	Avoidance	Drooper (I'm not OK)
Rebel	Delegates inappropriately	Blames	Suppression; Domination	Blamer (You're not OK)
Promoter	Does not suppor	Manipulates	Suppression; Domination	Blamer (You're not OK)

While our condominiums are "constructed" by the time we are seven years old, only the order of the floors is set. The amount of furnishing—the degree of energy—may change during our lives. This will occur with repeated visits to those sparsely furnished floors. When we go there time and time again, we bring more "furniture" and leave it there for our next visit.

Interestingly, once we have furnished a floor, it tends to stay furnished. Increased energy comes from experience and accepted invitations. The more we interact with others whose preferences are represented on our upper floors, the better those floors are furnished.

Putting Things Together

As we confront problems in our lives, we need to find an approach that works—one that will resolve the conflict and solve the problem. Here is a potential model for addressing problems:

- Define the problem.
- Acknowledge what, if any, additional information you need.
- Determine the urgency so that the situation can be considered with other priorities.
- Examine alternatives, looking at the pros and cons of each. (It is very important to consider both the positive and negative aspects, so you can see the benefits and the potential pitfalls as you make a decision.)
- Decide which approach you will take.
- Propose a plan to implement.
- Implement the plan.
- Consider how you will determine if your approach has been effective: Was the problem solved? Is the conflict resolved? (This is the step that may be ignored, but it is an important one.)

This straightforward approach has been proposed similarly by many others (Adams, 2001; Bolton, 1979; Gamble & Gamble, 1982; Maurer, 1991; Hersey, Blanchard, & Johnson, 2013). This model is very useful if you are a singular decision maker.

If it is more than your problem, then the approach takes on other layers. That is, when you might involve others, you will need to consider their perspectives and preferences, their professional/organizational and personal maturity, and the urgency of the situation.

Define the Problem

One of the first things we must do is decide who owns the problem (à la the Prologue). At times a frustrated staff member may barge into the office: "Here! You deal with this! I am out of patience and have other things that need my attention." You have had someone else's problem dropped on your doorstep. You can choose to deal with it—or not.

If you choose to deal with it, then you have assumed some ownership. You have agreed tacitly that you will be involved directly. Someone else's "monkey" (the problem) is now in your care.

On the other hand, you might agree to provide a cooling-off period for a decision to the *problem*, without delving further into the situation. You understand that the staff member has not been able to address the situation satisfactorily, but you acknowledge the problem is truly the staff member's. If you refuse to intervene, then you have set the pattern that the problem be addressed at the source, if possible.

Once the determination has been made regarding ownership of the problem, then the focus can shift to problem definition. From the outset, defining the problem should be done with an eye to solution.

The more contentious the situation, the more likely some people may want to *blame* or *attack*. Of course, this is more cathartic than productive and may lead to arguments that inhibit or prohibit moving ahead.

A useful way to define the problem is to describe the undesirable aspects of the situation.

- Given the previous anecdote from the staff member's viewpoint: "I cannot deal with her. She is constantly *playing*. She doesn't pay attention in our discussions." (The staff member is probably in Persister phase describing a Rebel's behavior, with the staff member having little Rebel energy or in distress to where he cannot access his Rebel floor.)
- From the other employee's perspective: "He didn't give me time to finish. The directions weren't clear." (This person has probably had all he can take of unexciting or mundane work, or boring discussion. She needs something more expressive and kinesthetic. She is into the second-degree distress of *blaming*.)

If the frustrated employee is unable to see the situation from the other person's perspective, it is unlikely that she will be able to define the problem any better. As a colleague, you might reflect your understanding of the situation: "You're frustrated that he can't stay on task and seems to want to play more than work." If you get, "Yes. That's it," then you have reflected what you have been told—understood the situation from the other person's point of view. If you get, "Not quite," then you may have to restate your understanding in other ways or ask for more information.

Here you might also offer her (privately): "Were there other things that happened before you saw the behavior that was unacceptable to you?" This approach invites your colleague to consider other things without your accepting ownership of the situation.

Secure Additional Necessary Information

We are often confronted with limited versions of the situation: People hear what they want to hear and report the version they want known. Adults are no more immune to this selective disclosure than are children.

When staff members cannot solve their problems and become frustrated, they look for allies or rescuers. One way to recruit an ally is to find someone who will agree with us and our perspective.

This agreement may come from our position or alliance within the organization for a common purpose or because we know our viewpoints match. As we fashion or reconfirm our alliance, we present the most positive information that invites others to see our position as tenable. That is, we say the things that put us in a favorable light and avoid description of things that may give us a negative pall.

In any event, most administrators are arbiters of what others lay at our feet. We rarely have an opportunity to observe situations unfolding first-hand.

One way to stay apprised is to be out and about during the workday, seeing the programs in operation—management by wandering around (Peters & Austin, 1985). In this way, you are familiar with what is happening and the people involved. (If you know folks by their names, they cannot be anonymous in your interactions with them.)

Determine the Urgency

"Failure to plan on your part does not constitute an emergency on my part!" is a placard or bumper sticker that might be displayed by someone who does not want others intruding needlessly. Another message that indicates failure to plan adequately is, "If I wanted it tomorrow, I'd have asked for it tomorrow."

Sometimes things become urgent for others, and they want our help immediately. Issues of *their* highest priority are presented to us with the expectation that we will see them with the same urgency.

The problems of other people may or may not have the same priority for us. We have to assess what else in our schedule may need more immediate attention, or we have to decide to put aside our priorities in deference to others. Of course, this means our work is postponed, and we may become frustrated or angry about having to work later or longer because of the interruption.

Leaders are challenged to assess their priorities constantly. Much of their interaction with others is initiated by others; hence, they may not truly be in control of their priorities.

Even if you have an *open-door* policy for addressing issues, close the door occasionally. Keep your door open only if you are "open." When you cannot be interrupted, do not allow others to intrude.

The more you rescue, the more people will come to you with their *emergencies*. Be very careful of responding, "I'll take care of it." No one knows better than you what you can and cannot do—and are willing to do.

ADAPTING

Examine Alternatives

With our experience, we develop patterns of dealing with similar issues. When we find a *tool* that works, we tend to use it again. Effective problem solving involves determining an appropriate approach for the current situation. (Again, having more tools at your disposal will give you a greater chance of selecting the right one.)

The amount of time we have to address a problem or issue may affect the resources we have to look at various options. Someone once said to me, "It's not an option if I will not do it." If we rush to judgment, we may overlook other viable possibilities.

Another factor that may interfere with our examining options is that we (mostly the Thinkers and Persisters among us) tend to look only at the negative consequences. It is important to look at the positive aspects of possibilities, too.

Looking at both celebrating the birthday and attending the professional meeting, we can see the following consequences:

- Positives
  - Fulfill professional expectations
  - Celebrate with child at a convenient time
- Negatives
  - May miss actual celebration
  - May disappoint child by not being at the actual party

With ample time, we can look at a number of possibilities. The number increases with the number of people involved and the permission we give ourselves to *color outside the lines*, or *think outside the box*.

(Those who may be *locked* into patterns may want to refer to other ways of conceptualizing [Adams, 2001; De Bono, 1970, 1985]. Also, it is important to note here that breaking away from established patterns is not only for Rebels. We all have the ability to be creative. However, some of us may have difficulty giving ourselves permission to consider other than established patterns or rules.)

Generating ideas can be done in a number of ways. Determining which method works best in a given situation depends on whether we are in the same place (co-located) at the same time (synchronously) or elsewhere (distant) at different times (asynchronously). With current computer software (e.g., Groupware, Zoom, discussion boards, etc.), we can work together synchronously or asynchronously, either at the same site or different locations. There are advantages and disadvantages to each method.

Working in the same location at the same time allows us to interpret the subtle body language we convey when we interact. This collaboration is limited by the people who can meet at a mutual location.

Using current technology allows us to branch out and involve people, regardless of where they are located. They can also respond at different times convenient to their schedules. What is missing, even with interactive televised exchanges, is the nonverbal *language* that helps with our understanding of what others convey. (Cf. Bull, 1983; Fast, 1970; Hall, 1959, 1966; and Mehrabian, 1971, 1972, for a more complete discussion of nonverbal language.)

Generating as many ideas as possible is useful if we have sufficient time to examine all of them. One *brainstorming* technique suggests we delay evaluation until all the ideas are presented. Using author anonymity permits us to assess the possibilities without attributing the preconceptions we may have about the people who suggest various ways to proceed. (This can be done electronically or by hand, using written ideas that are collated, summarized, and redistributed to the group.)

Decide on the Approach

Once we are satisfied that we have enough ideas, we can look at the pros and cons of each. We can balance the benefits and calculate the contingencies. Force-field analysis (Lewin, 1948) or other techniques can provide the structure for looking at alternatives by examining the *helping* and *hindering* forces. What we are looking for is the best alternative given the current circumstances of the situation.

There is no magic here. What may have worked at another time may not be appropriate now. In many situations, the wisdom of the group may work better than the decision of one individual.

Of course, this means that the group has the experience and knowledge to contribute and that the leader is willing to accept what the group offers. The leader may work either as a part of the group or as a supporter of a decision delegated to the group. (For deeper discussion of Situational Leadership, see Hersey, Blanchard & Johnson, 2013.)

When group participation is inappropriate (because of compressed time or inexperienced group members), the leader must decide. Here the leader's experience and knowledge is critical. Insufficient knowledge or unrelated experience will limit the options and the eventual decision.

One technique involving the group would be to classify the generated alternatives as *essential, desirable,* or *possible but impractical.* Codifying each type (5 for essential [E], 3 for desirable [D], and 1 for possible [P]) will facilitate categorizing the possibilities. Once that occurs, *advocacy* of any and all alternatives can proceed. Group members may want to say why one option will or will not work.

Table 12.2. Establishing Priorities

	Person 1	Person 2	Person 3	Person 4	Total
Alternative A	E	P	D	E	14
Alternative B	E	D	D	E	16
Alternative C	P	D	D	P	8
Alternative D	E	D	E	E	18
Alternative E	D	E	D	D	14

Legend: E=5, D=3, P=1

If we set a total of 12 (an average of *desirable* for all participants), then we can begin discussion/advocacy on Alternatives A, B, D, and E. These all averaged "desirable" or better by the people in the group (as seen above in Table 12.2).

When advocacy dwindles because of pre-established time limits or loss of energy, we can ask the group to list their top four (not a magic number) possibilities. Again, codifying may give us a tool for coalescing opinions (4 for the top choice, 3 for the second favorite, 2 for the third favorite, and 1 for the fourth favorite). From there, sums can be tallied, and the group can see the collective choice—the one with the highest total. (Note: Each rank may be used only once. No ties should be allowed. See Table 12.3.)

Table 12.3. Choosing Among Alternatives

	Person 1	Person 2	Person 3	Person 4	Total
Alternative A	4	3	3	1	11
Alternative B	3	4	4	2	13
Alternative D	3	3	2	4	10
Alternative E	1	1	1	3	6

Alternative B has the strongest support and should be the highest priority. If there are no mitigating circumstances (such as legal or budgetary considerations), then Alternative B should be implemented. If we are looking at our long-term goals and more than one can be addressed, then Alternative B is followed by A, C, and D, in that order. If B will not work for some reason (e.g., it is too costly), even though it seems to be the best solution, then A would be the next best solution to be implemented.

COMMUNICATING

Develop a Plan

The preferred alternative provides the direction for addressing the identified problem. The development of an implementation plan is—and should be—left to those who are charged with addressing the problem directly. Ownership of implementation specifics invests the stakeholders in the outcomes.

It is here that understanding interaction style preferences becomes important. Each of us has a preference for a particular style—*autocratic, democratic, benevolent,* or *laissez-faire* (presented in detail in Chapter 4 and discussed further in the Epilogue). Adopting an *individualistic* style (Kahler, 1982) gives one the full range of tools with which to work.

The leader who is energized and can go to the appropriate floor is able deal with others effectively. She or he will interact with Promoters and Imaginers autocratically, with Thinkers and Persisters democratically, with Harmonizers benevolently, and with Rebels in a laissez-faire manner. Interestingly, each of the other different people will respond positively with this approach if we communicate appropriately and use another's perceptual preference.

Table 12.4. Communication Preferences

Personality	Interaction Style	Channel	Perception
Harmonizer	Benevolent	Nurturative	Emotions
Thinker	Democratic	Requestive	Thoughts
Persister	Democratic	Requestive	Beliefs
Imaginer	Autocratic	Directive	Reflections
Rebel	Laissez Faire	Emotive	Reactions
Promoter	Autocratic	Directive	Actions

(Adapted with permission from Kahler [1996].)

The drawbacks or shortcomings are apparent when we do not get our own needs met and cannot get on our *elevator*, or if one or more of our *floors* are not furnished well enough for us to stay there for the period of time our colleagues may need or prefer.

Those are the times when we go to where *we* are most comfortable and familiar. If others accept our invitation to be there, too, we will be effective. If they reject the invitation, we will have to find another *venue* or postpone the interaction until we are more motivated (having met our individual needs).

If we have sufficient energy to *shift*, we can accommodate the preferences of others. The following examples reflect shifting (note the methods and perceptions):

- To a Harmonizer's perspective: "Barbara, you are very sensitive to this issue. How might we all work with each other?" (Nurturing, focusing on feelings)
- To a Thinker's perspective: "Alfred, you always have such good ideas. What do you think our options are?" (Requesting, focusing on thoughts)
- To a Persister's Perspective: "Matthew, this is a very important project. What do you believe the right approach is?" (Requesting, focusing on opinions)
- To a Imaginer's perspective: "Dorothy, tell me how you imagine the path we agreed to take." (Directing, focusing on reflections)
- To a Rebel's perspective: "Angie, what a great opportunity for your creative juices! Give me some of the super ideas you like by next Tuesday." (Emoting, focusing on reactions)
- To a Promoter's perspective: "Doug, you're the man [for the job]. Come up with an approach so we can get the job done." (Directing, focusing on action)

For most administrators, communicating with Barbara, Alfred, and Matthew will be most comfortable and familiar. Dorothy, Angie, and Doug may take a little to a lot more effort. For some of us, Angie and Doug are too difficult, and we will invite them elsewhere on a fairly regular basis. If they do not or cannot accept the invitation, we may have laid the groundwork for ongoing miscommunication, leading to continual conflict.

Ongoing rejection of communication invitations can lead to a predictable pattern, a *dance*—an interaction with a cadence but lack of progress:

- Matthew (Persister): "Why don't you start with polling the staff for their ideas?"
- Angie (Rebel): "Yeah, that might be a good way to start, but I am not sure they will like having to give up their free time."
- Matthew: "Well, why don't ask them for the times when they are available to work with you?"
- Angie: "That might work, but I would need to spend time with them explaining the project."
- Matthew: "Why don't you . . . ?"
- Angie: "Yes, but . . ."
- Matthew: "Why don't you . . . ?"
- Angie: "Yes, but . . ."

You can hear the *beat* and see the lack of progress. When these two people leave the interaction with nothing really accomplished, Matthew might say to himself: *"What is it with Angie? Is she so dense that she can't see how important this project is? Why do I have to explain everything to her?"*

Angie's reaction might be: *"I don't like this project. I don't like Matthew's constantly trying to get me to take over. I don't want to do it. Anyway, he hasn't given me all the resources I need."*

How Do You Know?

Trying to see a situation from another person's perspective indicates: (1) you are willing to put aside your preferences for a time, and (2) you understand another's preferences and motivation. Process Communication gives us the tools to interpret preferences and motivation through the words, tones, postures, gestures, and facial expression people use.

(Another way of determining one's preferences and motivation is through a profile generated from responses to a preference survey—the *Personality Pattern Inventory©*.) The predictable patterns of distress behaviors tell us what people want and what drives them. If we listen to the words that people use, we can understand their perceptual preferences and moving to the appropriate channel. (See Table 12.5.)

Table 12.5. **Personality, Word Choices, & Communication Channels**

Personality	Word Examples	Channel
Harmonizer	Emotions: love, sense, feel, care, happy, sad, comfortable, family	Nurturative
Thinker	Thoughts: think, judge, conclude, structure, time, logic(al)	Requestive
Persister	Opinions: believe, value, judge, important, crucial	Requestive
Imaginer	Reflections: (passive voice: "It seems . . ." "It occurred to me . . .")	Directive
Rebel	Reactions: like, dislike, enjoy, hate	Emotive
Promoter	Actions: do, tell, finish, "bottom line"	Directive

(Adapted with permission from Kahler [1996].)

Implement the Decision

Once the plan of operation is determined, key staff will implement the plan. Again, if those who are charged with the implementation have contributed to the decision, they are likely to be more enthusiastic about how well it is implemented. Owners of the decision are more invested in its positive outcomes. That is, if I help to make a decision, I want it to work well.

Determine the Success

Administrators often look to their titular authority and assume their decision has been implemented and has been effective because they made the decision. To verify their authority, they should move past the assumption that organizational status is sufficient to cause action. It is more realistic to look to the compliance and enthusiasm of staff.

Further, it is important to assess if the decision is effective. Just because a decision has been made does not mean it will accomplish the planned outcome.

If we set out in a given direction knowing it will take a certain amount of time to get where we are going, we need to check our progress periodically. Pre-establishing benchmarks or check points is a useful way to see if we are headed in the right direction and are making steady progress.

If our goal is Memphis and we head west on Interstate 40 from Nashville, we should "achieve" Memphis (about 200 miles away) in about three hours. If we drive the speed limit and there are no detours or traffic clogs, what do we do if there is "no" Memphis in four hours? Do we continue driving? (Of course not, but some might continue.) Do we stop and ask for directions? (Not a bad idea!) Do we check our progress? (A really good option.)

With organizational programs, we see some inertia. Movement causes further movement—whether or not there are reasons to check if the movement is productive. Conversely, lack of movement tends to perpetuate no movement, that is, nothing changes without great effort. (This is very similar to the physical law that says a body in motion tends to stay in motion, and a body at rest tends to stay at rest unless acted upon by an outside force.)

Effective leaders are the forces to stimulate change—encouraging people to go places they would not choose by themselves (Barker, 1999). It is important to be sure the signposts are in place before we set out. We need to specify our indicators for success as we put our plan in operation and look to those indicators as the program unfolds, making adjustments as necessary. This is *task focus*.

A sometimes-lost but equally important component is whether the people involved in a project are satisfied—whether their morale is high enough to keep them motivated to the benefit of the organization (and for themselves). This *relationship focus* when combined with *task focus* yields the potential for *individualistic leadership* (the opportunity to express high degrees of concern for both outcomes and the satisfaction that leads to high morale).

The Process Communication Model gives us the interaction *signposts* for success. If we know what the signals of distress (unfulfilled need) are, we can make appropriate adjustments in our style (if the distress is related to the project). Distress in one's personal life can interfere, but leaders should be cautious about trespassing without permission into the lives of their colleagues.

If you see the following patterns, with what type of person are you interacting and what might you do professionally? (A formula you might use is to deal with the behavior first, then try to find the appropriate channel and perception to *communicate*—to reach understanding. See Appendix A for the personality types and suggestions for assisting each to stay energized and stay out of distress.)

People in distress are not as open to communication as those who are motivated—that is, unfulfilled needs motivate a person to focus on fulfilling those needs, mostly with negative behaviors. As our energy is focused on getting our needs met, we have little energy to focus on what others may need.

We cannot *shift* to other *frames of preference* (see Appendix A) until our own needs are satisfied, and until we regenerate the energy to be motivated to look beyond ourselves. Knowing negative behaviors allows a leader to understand what others are experiencing and to interact with them in meaningful ways.

Table 12.6 encapsulates the Frames of Preference for the personality phases leaders are likely to see in colleagues, students, and others in their professional (and personal) lives. These *frames* provide indicators for distress and suggestions for both intervening in distress and for preventing distress. (A more extensive list is found in Appendix B.)

Your effectiveness as a leader will be found in your ability to communicate—the degree to which you are able to get others to understand your perspective and message. Further, your leadership will be measured by your ability to guide others to places they would not choose by themselves.

Table 12.6. Frames of Preference (© Kahler Communications, Inc.)

Type	Harmonizer	Thinker	Persister	Imaginer	Rebel	Promoter
Strengths	Compassionate, sensitive, warm	Logical, responsible, organized	Conscientious, dedicated, observant	Imaginative, reflective, calm	Spontaneous, creative, playful	Adaptable, persuasive, charming
Perceptions	Feelings	Thoughts	Beliefs	Reflections (inactions)	Reactions (likes & dislikes)	Actions
Needs	Acceptance of self; sensory stimuli	Recognition of (good) work; time structure	Recognition of (valuable) work; convictions	Solitude	Contact	Incidence
First-Degree Distress	Wants to please others; overadapts	Expects perfect self; overthinks for others	Expects perfect others; focuses on what's wrong	Has to be strong to survive	Tries harder; feigns lack of understanding	Expects others to be strong
Second-Degree Distress	Appears confused; makes mistakes; invites others to criticize	Critical about time, fairness, responsibility issues	Preaches, crusades, critical about details	Withdraws; is embarrassed; overly shy	Blames others; acts irresponsibly; invites negative sanctions	Manipulates; break rules; sets up negative drama
Intervention	Nurture; stroke verbally	Clarify issues; provide facts/data	Acknowledge beliefs; recognize value of work	Allow private time/own space; direct to action	Interact playfully, with high energy	Focus on exciting ways of doing things; provide lots of activity
Prevention	Comfortable workplace; group activities; personal connection	Clear time frames; rewards for accomplishments	Obvious rules & structure; projects that appeal to belief system	Projects to be done alone; permission to withdraw; limited group activities	Playful contact; acceptance of play before work	Short-term assignments; positive competition; physical involvement

POINTS TO PONDER

- The causes or sources of conflict should be diagnosed carefully.
- In dealing with conflict, effective leaders need to adapt the way they see things.
- They need to *shift* to the preferences of the parties in conflict to communicate effectively.

REFERENCES

Adams, J. L. (2001). *Conceptual blockbusting: A guide to better ideas* (4th ed.). New York, NY: Basic Books.

Barker, J. L. (1999). *Leadershift: Five lessons for leaders in the 21st century.* St. Paul, MN: Star Thrower Productions (video).

Barnard, C. I. (1938). *The functions of the executive.* Cambridge, MA: Harvard University Press.

Blake, R. R., & Mouton, J. S. (1985). *The Managerial Grid III: A new look at the classic that has boosted productivity and profits for thousands of corporations worldwide.* Houston, TX: Gulf Publishing Co.

Bolton, R. (1979). *People skills: How to assert yourself, listen to others, and resolve conflicts.* Englewood Cliffs, NJ: Prentice-Hall.

Bull, P. (1983). *Body movement and interpersonal communication.* New York, NY: Wiley.

De Bono, E. (1970). *Lateral thinking: Creativity step by step.* New York, NY: Harper & Row.

De Bono, E. (1985). *Six thinking hats.* Toronto, ON: Little, Brown and Co.

Fast, J. (1970). *Body language.* New York, NY: Pocket Books.

Gamble, T. K., & Gamble, M. (1982). *Contacts: Communicating interpersonally.* New York, NY: Random House.

Glatthorn, A. A., & Adams, H. R. (1983). *Listening your way to management success.* Glenview, IL: Scott, Foresman and Co.

Hall, E. T. (1959). *The silent language.* Garden City, NY: Doubleday.

Hall, E. T. (1966). *The hidden dimension.* Garden City, NY: Doubleday.

Hersey, P., Blanchard, K., & Johnson, D. E. (2013). *Management of organizational behavior: Utilizing human resources* (10th ed.). Upper Saddle River, NJ: Pearson.

Kahler, T. (1982). *Personality Pattern Inventory validation studies.* Little Rock, AR: Kahler Communications, Inc.

Kahler, T. (1996). *The advanced Process Communication seminar.* Little Rock, AR: Kahler Communications, Inc.

Lewin, K. (1948). *Resolving social conflicts: Selected papers on group dynamics* (ed. by G. W. Lewin). New York, NY: Harper.

Maurer, R. E. (1991). *Managing conflict: Tactics for school administrators.* Needham Heights, MA: Allyn & Bacon.

Mehrabian, A. (1971). *Silent messages.* Belmont, CA: Wadsworth Publishing Co.
Mehrabian, A. (1972). *Nonverbal communication.* Chicago, IL: Aldine-Atherton.
Metcalf, H. C., & Urwick, L. (Eds.). (1940). *Dynamic administration: The collected papers of Mary Parker Follett.* New York, NY: Harper & Row.
Ouchi, W. G. (1982). *Theory Z: How American business can meet the Japanese challenge.* New York, NY: Avon.
Peters, T., & Austin, N. (1985). *A passion for excellence: The leadership difference.* New York, NY: Random House.

Chapter Thirteen

Changing Leadership Behavior

As leaders decide to move the organization in a different direction, they set up a series of dynamics for change. Recognizing that change is uncomfortable is one of the biggest realities to face. Part of the change is what the leader will do differently. There will be a different light bulb in place, one that requires a new tool.

CHANGING BEHAVIOR

Organizations progress as they translate their purpose into goals, change their goals in objectives, change objectives into action, and evaluate the results of those actions as they relate to the success of the organization. Change would appear to be simple process (Lewin, 1947): unfreezing from the current position, moving to a new position, and freezing there, until a reason emerges to change again.

During the process, forces emerge to either help or hinder change. An analysis of balance between these forces can help facilitate change or postpone it. These forces may be inter- or intrapersonal (idiographic), or organizational (nomothetic) (cf. Getzels & Guba, 1957). The idiographic forces may precede or override the nomothetic ones. However, the personal considerations are crucial to communicate effectively. Without that understanding, leaders may miss important cues to transmit messages.

Change may occur in four sequential stages (Hersey, Blanchard & Johnson 2013). First comes a change in knowledge—awareness of something new. Without new information, one is limited to what he or she knows currently. Next would come a change in attitude—interpreting the new knowledge and responding to it. Third would be a change in individual behavior—doing something different or differently. With a change in individual attitude and behavior would come the fourth stage, change in group (or organizational) behavior. Each higher level subsumes the previous one.

Movement through the first three stages would be personal, or internal. The process can stop at any stage if the individual does not embrace what comes next. For example, if I do not see the value in the new information, my attitude is negative, and I am unlikely to change my behavior:

> I facilitated a Dental Hygiene for Teachers workshop some years ago. The dentist who provided the technical information offered that there were two reasons for dental disease—bacterial and nutritional.
>
> It takes a colony of bacteria about 24 hours to grow in the mouth. Therefore, if you clean your mouth completely once a day, you will eliminate the bacterial cause of dental disease.
>
> A kindergarten teacher in the group asked if one should brush three times a day. The dentist went through the information again, adding guidance about brushing and flossing. The teacher persisted with what she knew about brushing —one should brush three times a day. She was not convinced about the new information.
>
> The likelihood is that she did not change her attitude about dental hygiene, nor did she change her individual behavior. She probably continued to brush three times a day.

As the teacher in the example was unconvinced, it is likely that her dental hygiene lessons to her students were to brush three times a day. Also, she probably did not change her individual behavior and was, therefore, unlikely to add the new information to changing group behavior. Therefore, the change process was stalled at the knowledge level.

This is one example of maintaining the status quo, or system justification. This theory "holds that—to varying degrees—people are motivated (often non-consciously) to defend, justify, and bolster aspects of the societal status quo, and that this is an important psychological and ideological contributor to resistance to change" (Jost, 2015, p. 622). Without adequate impetus, change is unlikely.

If change is important to progress toward organizational goals, what can be done? The predominant strategies are (cf. Dent & Galloway, 1999):

- education;
- participation;
- facilitation;
- negotiation;
- manipulation; and
- coercion.

Obviously, some of these strategies are positive, and others can be perceived as negative. The success of change lies in a blending of the personal and organizational dimensions into transactional behavior (Getzels & Guba, 1957). If behavior is, as Lewin (1947) suggested, a function of personality and experience, leaders would be most effective when considering the interaction of personality and experience (current with regard to the organization and the applicants' work histories when reviewing what the workforce brings with them).

Personality, the heart of Process Communication, is the more elusive to interpret. We have many theories at our disposal (cf. Costa & McCrae, 1994; Keirsey, 1978; Myers, 1962).

The reality is that personality does not change (Costa & McCrae, 1994); however, individuals can adapt their behaviors to interact with others effectively. Failure to adapt can lead to miscommunication and lack of achievement. Herein lies the utility of the PCM—understanding oneself and others facilitates effective communication. However, one must be willing to put in the energy to change.

REINFORCING TRAINING

Time, money, and energy spent on updating knowledge and skills need to show the all-important *return on investment*. Simply showing up for training and being involved to varying degrees may spark interest at the time, but the effects can wane very quickly without ongoing practice and feedback (Averell & Heathcote, 2011).

It has been estimated that:

- less than half of the skills and information presented in training sessions will be transferred to the job unless there is follow-up;
- within six months, as much as 75% of the training will be lost without follow-up; and
- after one year, some participants will retain as little as 10–15% of what was presented without reinforcement. (BLR, 2018)

Coaching, mentoring, and self-reflection are some of the ways to reinforce training (Moran, n.d.). Organizations must be intentional to maximize the benefits of providing professional development. This may be very similar to internships, where supervisors (akin to mentors and coaches) are present to observe and redirect when necessary. Having someone in the organization to reinforce the training or regular access to experts is imperative for lasting behavioral change.

POINTS TO PONDER

- Decisions to change must be intentional.
- Leaders must recognize that change is uncomfortable.
- Reinforcing training is crucial for long-lasting effect.

REFERENCES

Averell, L., & Heathcote, A. (2011). The form of the forgetting curve and the fate of memories. *Journal of Mathematical Psychology, 55*(1), 25–35.

BLR. (2018). Reinforcing your employee training, available at: www.blr.com/training tips/training-program-reinforcement (accessed May 7, 2018).

Costa, P. T. Jr., & McCrae, R. R. (1994). Set like plaster? Evidence for the stability of adult personality. In Heatherton, T. F. and Weinberger, J. L. (Eds). *Can personality change?* Washington, DC: American Psychological Association, pp. 21–40.

Dent, E. B., & Galloway, S. G. (1999). Challenging "resistance to change." *The Journal of Applied Behavioral Science, 35*(1), 25–41.

Getzels, J. W., & Guba, E. G. (1957). Social behavior and the administrative process. *The School Review, 65*(4), 423–441, available at: www.jstor.org/stable/1083752 (accessed February 10, 2018).

Hersey, P., Blanchard, K., & Johnson, D. E. (2013). *Management of organizational behavior: Utilizing human resources* (10th ed.). Upper Saddle River, NJ: Pearson.

Jost, J. T. (2015). Resistance to change: A social psychological perspective. *Social Research, 82*(3), 607–636.

Keirsey, D. (1978). *Please understand me II: Temperament, character, intelligence*. Green Valley Lake, CA: Prometheus Nemesis Book.

Lewin, K. (1947). Frontiers in group dynamics: Concept, method, and reality in social science; social equilibria and social change. *Human Relations, 1*(1), 5–41, available at: https://doi.org/10.1177/001872674700100103 (accessed February 10, 2018).

Moran, L. (n.d.). Strategic reinforcement: The value of making change stick, available at: www.rpi.edu/dept/hr/docs/StrategicTrainingReinforcement.pdf (accessed May 7, 2018).

Myers, I. B. (1962). *Myers-Briggs Type Indicator*. Palo Alto, CA: Consulting Psychologists Press.

Epilogue

Installing the Capstones

Inspecting the finished product and making necessary adjustments are benchmarks of effective builders. If the joints are misaligned or there are paint spatters, it is important that the builder modify the work to a higher standard.

As a leader, you might do similar inspections. Following an interaction, you might ask:

- What was the objective of the meeting?
- Did we accomplish the objective?
  - What techniques helped in accomplishing the objective?
  - What barriers did we fail to overcome?
- What might we have done differently to achieve a better result?

Affirming what worked well and changing what did not are important aftermaths. Many want to focus only on the negative results, and others want to avoid analyzing altogether. Acknowledging what has worked is a key to giving yourself well-earned credit and reinforcing effective leadership.

Drawing on the tools and techniques of Process Communication, we can use an Assessing Matrix© (Kahler, 2010). Here we see that each personality type falls into one of four quadrants (remembering that we are a composite of all personalities). One axis describes how we interact, from *Involved* to *Withdrawn*; the other axis describes the degree to which we are motivated *Intrinsically* or *Extrinsically*.

We see that the personality types that are motivated from within with varying degrees of involvement. Those who prefer to be more involved (Harmonizers) enjoy the company of others and prefer to work in groups. Those who prefer less involvement (Thinkers and Persisters) would rather interact either one-on-one or alone.

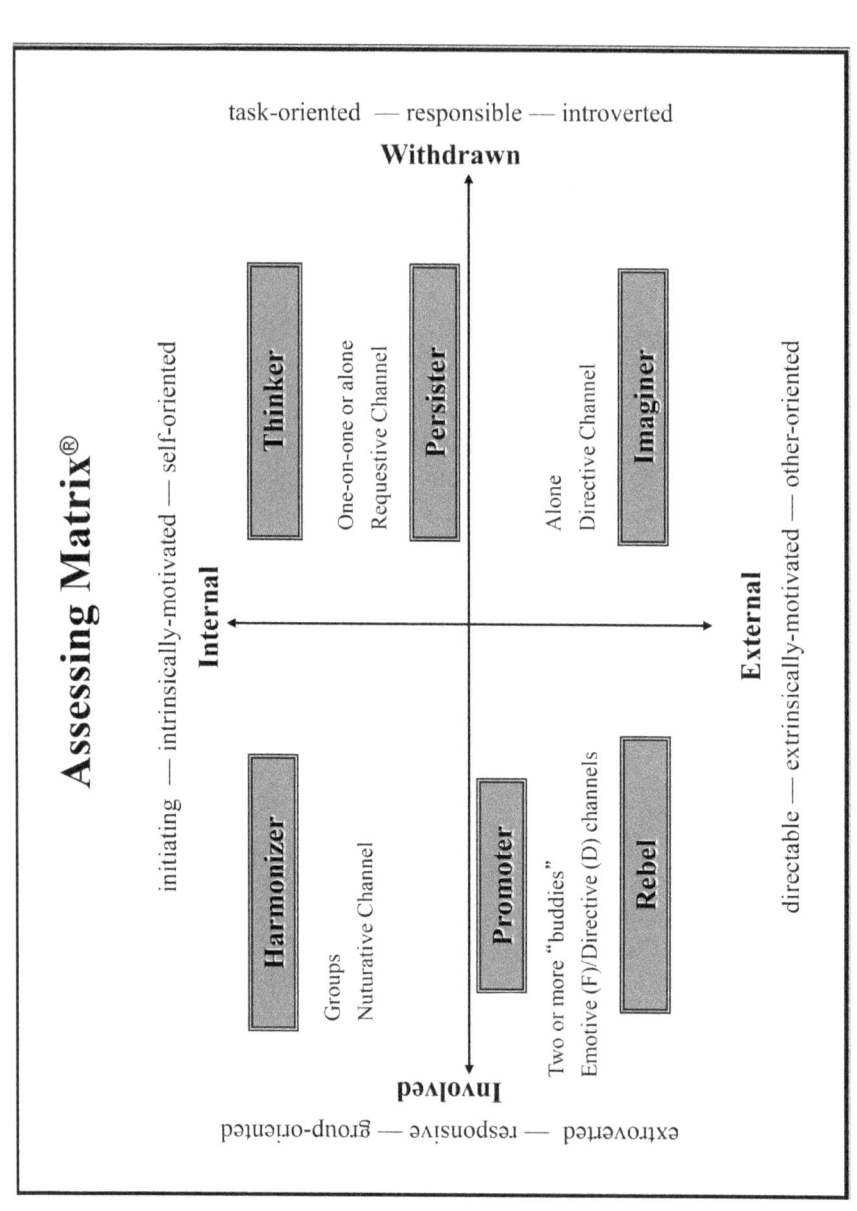

Figure Epilogue.1. Assessing Matrix. *Source:* Kahler Communications Inc.

Those who prefer to be less involved with others tend to be more *task-oriented*. Conversely, those who prefer greater involvement are more *relationship-oriented*.

The challenge for most leaders is *shifting* to interact effectively with those (Imaginers, Rebels, and Promoters) who need external motivation—a quality less common among leaders. However, many leaders may have sparsely furnished "floors" where they might interact with those who prefer external motivation. That is, the tools available on those floors are simple. Not used very often, they may feel awkward in the hands of those preferring more familiar techniques.

Below is a situation we might use as a capstone (a component that completes the roof of a building and makes it sound) to the communication and interaction framework discussed above.

> A large organization had re-roofed one of its buildings. It leaked after the first serious rain after the project was completed.
>
> The contract had gone to the lowest bidder, and the contractor had neglected to install capstones. (The installation was neither specified in the contract, nor did the contractor follow an industry standard.)

It was an important lesson: Capstones are critical if roofs are to be sound—and the lowest bidder is not necessarily the best.

The following vignette is an example of a problem that might arise in an organization. While it may seem simple or something that is unlikely to happen, problems like these do occur.

> You are manager of a major division of your organization. The company is successful and supportive of you as the division administrator.
>
> One of your key employess has refused to obey a reasonable request of his supervisor. The employee would not do the work, as requested by the supervisor. Instead, the work was done in a different fashion from what was prescribed.
>
> The supervisor referred the employee to you for being insubordinate. You have asked the employee, the supervisor, and the union representative to meet with you. The union rep is very busy and seems agitated at interrupting the workday to attend the meeting.
>
> The supervisor oversees what has been a very orderly operation, up until now. The production is smooth, workers have specific assignments, and there are specific guidelines for how work is to be done.
>
> The supervisor insists on strict compliance with guidelines because of the belief that it promotes good discipline in the workers and limits mistakes. The workers respond by doing neat and precise work. They also perform at above-average levels on industry standards.
>
> The employee preferred to do things his way because it was faster and more fun. The supervisor refused to accept his rationale. The supervisor would not

yield to the explanation that it is more efficient. The issue of the employee's wanting the production process to be more fun was besides the point.

How might you deal with this situation to resolve the problem(s)? Of course, first decide whose "monkey" it is?

The supervisor is upset because the established procedures were abridged. The union rep does not want to interrupt the workday for something that did not need union involvement. The employee wants special treatment. None of these people can *resolve* the situation by himself or herself or among themselves and need your assistance.

If you were Dorothy (the Imaginer) or Doug (the Promoter), you would most likely take an *autocratic* (directive) approach. However, Dorothy might try to avoid a confrontation unless she *shifted* to some other part of her personality. She would be uncomfortable with everyone in distress and having the prospect of dealing with them face-to-face.

> Doug: "I understand that Supervisor has established guidelines. They seem reasonable, and employees are obliged to follow reasonable rules and directives.
>
> "Union Rep, please assist us by telling your member that rules are meant to be followed.
>
> "Employee, follow Supervisor's directions.
>
> "Supervisor, tell me if there are other things we need to do."

This matter-of-fact approach encourages others to respond directly. It works best with those who require direction, structure, or training. It does not encourage group interaction or feedback. It invites rebellious behavior.

The directive nature will probably upset the Union Rep further. The Union Rep might respond in one of two ways: (1) *"Why do I need to be here? A phone call or a note could have accomplished the same thing?"* Or (2) *"How dare you tell me what to do? Just who do you think you are?"* This will set up a battle with the Union Rep either way.

The employee is likely to feel disengaged and powerless: (1) *"They never listen to me. Why bother? I am always wrong."* Or (2) *"OK! If that's the way it is, I'll do it, but I'll get them—all of them—some other way."*

The employee may seem to comply, but the perceived incompatibility—the conflict—has not been resolved. As a result, the conflict is likely to resurface in other ways. (Overt or covert sabotage is within the realm of possibilities.)

If you were Matthew (the Persister) or Alfred (the Thinker), you would take a *democratic* approach. However, you would find it important to emphasize the rules or that the employee do what is right or expected.

Matthew/Alfred: "I understand we have a problem with Employee's not following how Supervisor expects assignments to be done.

"Supervisor, will you explain your guidelines and why they are important?

"Employee, will you listen carefully and ask questions about anything you do not understand?

"Union Rep, will you support us?"

The *democratic* administrator attempts to involve all the participants. She or he encourages them to be goal-oriented. In this case, the goal of the supervior and the focus of the administrator is that employees comply with the rules. However, this approach does not allow employees to diverge from the rules, or accommodate those who may not understand their responsibilities or who may be unwilling to comply. The supervisor's rules will be reinforced (but may be brought into question).

The Union Rep may still be confused or upset at the intrusion into the workday: *"I am not exactly sure why they needed me here just to ask me to support their rules. They could have done it over the telephone or in a note."*

The employee may get into a *try hard* position: *"Well, if Supervisor had explained it better, I would have done the work differently."* Or engage in "Yes, but . . .": *"I understand the rules, but I prefer to do things that work better for me."*

If you were Barbara (the Harmonizer), you would attempt to be highly empathic with everyone. You want harmony and would choose a *benevolent* approach.

Barbara: "I see we seem to have a problem. Let's see if we can work something out so everyone will be happy.

"Employee, you know things would be OK, if you would just follow Supervisor's rules."

"Union Rep, I am sure you can help Employee to understand how to get along with Supervisor's procedures."

"Supervisor, might there be a way to accept Employee's preferences?"

This approach focuses on people and attempts to resolve problems in a nurturing and accepting way. It works well with people who are predominantly feeling-oriented and who need unconditional acceptance. It is disadvantageous if the task is ignored. That is, people may *feel* better, but the problem may only be suppressed or ignored.

The employee may feel patronized, and the issue of personal preference has not been addressed, other than an allusion to following the rules. The employee might say, *"Yeah, I guess I can do that,"* but might not stick to the *agreement*.

The union rep has not been engaged in the solution, but has been directed, albeit gently, to support the organization. The situation has been avoided. *"Excuse me,"* the union rep might say. *"Can we talk about the problem here?"*

Without unconditional support for the rules, the supervisor may feel discounted. *"No, I will not accept Employee's reasoning. The rules were known from the first day. They are posted, and employees acknowledged they understood them during orientation."*

The *benevolent* approach may have inflamed the situation. The problem has not been resolved.

If you were Angie (the Rebel), you would take a *laissez-faire* approach. You would be non-directive and want the participants to accept responsibility for resolving the problem.

> Angie: "Well, Employee, I hear you have a problem.
>
> "Supervisor, you don't really need my help . . . now do you?
>
> "Union Rep, thanks for comin' in. I know you can help."

This detached attitude will have everyone doing some serious head scratching—wondering about the purpose of the meeting and what the direction is. The *laissez-faire* approach works well for individuals who can and are willing to accept responsibility for their actions; it invites independence and creativity. It does not, however, provide direction for people who may need structure and guidance.

The employee may think: *"Well, yeah I have a problem. What do you think I'm doin' here?"*

The supervisor may stay silent and acknowledge: *"Well, yes. I suppose I can handle it."* Or the supervisor may reassert the frustration that prompted the meeting: *"Yes, I do need your help. I have tried all I know how to do."* And may even become argumentative: *"Why do you think I came here in the first place?"*

The union rep may try to redirect the administrator and seek more information: *"Precisely, what is it that you would recommend I do?"*

Again, the problem is not resolved. In fact, another layer may have been added—lack of communication.

If communication is understanding a message in the way the sender intended and responding appropriately, we might consider the *individualistic* approach (see Chapter 4) to the situation. This requires a person to *shift* to a different style when necessary. Moreover, it requires that we consider *HOW* we communicate, as well as *WHAT* we communicate (Kahler, 2010).

Epilogue

Of course, we want others to own the problem that is rightly theirs and participate in the resolution. As we look at a possible scenario, we want to be sure to act as a facilitator rather than appearing to be all-knowing or accepting the problem as ours.

Most administrators will begin to define a problem by turning first to the one who presents the need for resolution. Another way to proceed is to start with the person with the least amount of *power* (if that is a different person). You, as the manager, will try to *lead* the others to a resolution of the problem.

Shifter: "Employee, can you tell me why you are here?"

Employee: "I dunno. Supervisor's pickin' on me."

Shifter: "Supervisor doesn't understand what you are saying."

Employee: "Yeah . . . but I can't do my work the way I want."

Shifter: "Would there be a problem if you could do your work your way?"

Employee: "Nope."

The leader has reflected that she or he understands what the employee has said. Nothing has been done yet to resolve the situation. Given that the employee has been understood, it is likely she or he will be engaged in the eventual resolution—at least, she or he has not been discounted or discarded from the process.

Many times administrators may presume the employee is wrong; otherwise, why would the supervisor have broached the situation in the first place? That approach does little more than exclude the employee from the outset. If we want employees (or others) to change their behavior, we have to include them in the process or the decision making. Without that involvement, there can be no *integration* or ownership in the final decision.

Shifter: "Union Rep, what do you see the problem to be?"

Union Rep: "I'm not sure, but I think it is an issue of following Supervisor's rules."

Shifter: "It appears to be the case to me, too."

Union Rep: "I am not exactly sure how I can help."

Shifter: "Will you help Employee follow through on whatever we all decide?"

Union Rep: "Oh! I think I can support that."

Asking for the union rep's help without being demanding, demeaning, or challenging the union rep's authority will go a long way to resolving the situation. If the union rep is part of the solution, you may have recruited an ally.

Shifter: "Supervisor, as I understand the situation, Employee prefers to do things different from your expectations and directives. Is that correct?"

Supervisor: "Yes."

Shifter: "Is there anything else that is going on with Employee's work?"

Supervisor: "Not that I am aware of. Usually, Employee's work is good to excellent."

Shifter: "Other than to enforce your rules and to reiterate them when necessary, have you talked with Employee about the lapse?"

Supervisor: "I've tried. Rules are rules, and these expectations seem reasonable to me. Also, they were discussed during initial orientation."

Shifter: "How do you propose to proceed?"

Teacher: "I simply want Employee to do the work as expected, with no variation."

Everyone has had a chance to participate, starting with the one with the least amount of power. The leader has engaged everyone without taking sides or trying to resolve someone else's problem. Everyone seems to agree what the problem is—failure to follow rules.

Shifter: "Everyone seems to agree. The issue is following Supervisor's expectations for how work should be done.

"Employee, you would prefer to do it your way.

"Union Rep, you are willing to support what we decide.

"Supervisor, you want your rules obeyed.

"So, how might we resolve this issue? Employee, what is your suggestion?"

Employee: "I dunno. Doing my work only one way isn't fun. It's boring."

Shifter: "Supervisor, do you see another option?"

Supervisor: "Well, if following established procedures is the problem, perhaps we can examine alternatives?"

Shifter: "Hmm! That sounds like a plan. Employee, will that work for you?"

Employee: "I guess, but I want to be part of a group that looks at possible alternatives."

Shifter: "In the meantime, you will follow Supervisor's rules. OK?"

Employee: "Yeah. I guess."

Shifter: "Union Rep, is this something you can support?"

Union Rep: "Sounds good to me."

Shifter: "OK. It is my understanding that Employee will work according to established procedure, and that Employee will talk with Supervisor about any problems as they arise rather than disobeying rules. Supervisor will involve Employee in a discussion group to consider possible alternatives. Is that OK with everyone?"

If you feel any misunderstanding still remains, you may want to write a "memorandum (or letter) of understanding" to all parties to reiterate the agreement. In that way, everyone has a written version of the oral agreement, which may be used should a similar problem arise. (Email will work, too. It will give you a record of the communication.)

It would seem that the immediate problem has been resolved integratively—both parties (here, the supervisor and the employee) contributing with neither party losing. Since no one has lost, the situation is unlikely to re-emerge. It is a win-win solution, or resolution: The supervisor's rules remain intact, the employee has clear direction and an opportunity to provide input, and the union rep has been involved in the discussion to support the employee.

A side note here: the employee is showing signs of distress. Blaming shows lack of need fulfillment (playful contact here). This employee might not be in a job that will be motivating, unless the work can be more fun, or if the employee can "play" beforehand.

Not all problems can be resolved creatively or integratively, and attempting to use *integration* takes longer. Resolving problems integratively is longer lasting (perhaps, even permanent) than ignoring, suppressing, dominating, or compromising.

POINTS TO PONDER

- Each of us has preferred ways of doing things, of handling conflicts in specific ways.
- If everyone involved in a conflict sees things in the same way and communicates similarly, then resolving the conflict moves more easily. If perceptual and communication styles are different, broaching the conflict is more problematic.

- Understanding the differences gives a leader clues as to how to communicate effectively.
- *Shifting* into other *frames of preference* is the key to effective conflict resolution.

REFERENCE

Kahler, T. (2010). *Process Communication management seminar*. Little Rock, AR: Kahler Communications, Inc.

Appendix A
Frames of Preference

Presented in this section you will find a review of the character strengths, perceptual preferences, main motivators, and distress patterns for each of the personality types you encountered earlier. Included also are extended lists of suggestions for each personality to the keep batteries charged and remain energized. For you, the list suggests how you can stay in a place where you are motivated. For others whose personalities and needs you understand, the lists give you ways you can connect with them, intervene in their distress, and suggest to them ways in which they can stay energized and motivated. (Adapted with permission from Kahler, T. [1996]. *The advanced Process Communication seminar.* Little Rock, AR: Kahler Communications, Inc.)

	Harmonizer
Character Strengths:	*Compassionate, sensitive, warm*
Perceptual Preferences:	Feelings, emotions, sensations
Motivating Factors:	Personal attention/appreciation; sensory satisfaction
Distress Patterns:	
First Degree:	Wants to please others; overadapts to people/situations
Second Degree:	Appears confused; makes mistakes; invites criticism
Needs Fulfillment:	Creating own "nest" at home and work
	Arranging for personal recognition and acceptance
	Working with groups of people who appreciate you
	Volunteering for projects with help others
	Spending special time with children (yours or others)
	Getting massage or back rub
	Keeping fresh flowers available to be seen and smelled
	Having special pictures of loved ones to be seen by self and others
	Using incense, aromatic candles, and/or potpourri
	Taking bubble baths
	Having lunch with a close friend/spouse regularly
	Using best china, linen, and silver without need of special occasion
	Strolling through fragrance section of department store
	Buying your favorite cologne/scent
	Telling and receiving messages of "I love you!"
	Giving and receiving hugs
	Walking in the garden, forest, rain, etc.
	"Dressing" for dinner

	Thinker
Character Strengths:	*Logical, responsible, organized*
Perceptual Preferences:	Thoughts, ideas, facts, information
Motivating Factors:	Recognition for work; time structure
Distress Patterns:	
First Degree:	Wants to be perfect; overcontrols; delegates poorly or not at all
Second Degree:	Becomes critical about fairness, responsibility, time; attacks others who do not think clearly
Needs Fulfillment:	Setting priorities
	Focusing on doing what is most important
	Arranging for acknowledgment of accomplishments
	Having clear times frames and responsibilities
	Making "to do" lists and crossing off what has been completed
	Keeping a journal
	Using an appointment book/calendar (paper or electronic)
	Displaying tangible recognition of work—certificates, plaques, etc.
	Creating awards for family for accomplished tasks/responsibilities
	Taking on tasks with tangible outcomes of completion
	Attending workshop to increase skill or expertise/data base
	Having a hobby with tangible outcomes—gardening, etc.
	Rewarding self with "Certificate of Accomplishment"
	Having a trusted "sounding board" for ideas or proposed projects

	Persister
Character Strengths:	*Conscientious, dedicated, observant*
Perceptual Preferences:	Beliefs, opinions, values
Motivating Factors:	Recognition for work; acceptance of convictions
Distress Patterns:	
First Degree:	Wants others to be perfect; focuses on what is wrong
Second Degree:	Frustrated with differing opinions; preaches/crusades about things of perceived importance; is suspicious; criticizes details and lack of commitment
Needs Fulfillment:	Joining/increasing religious activities/affiliations
	Discussing religion, politics, and current events
	Sharing personal values and beliefs with trusted colleagues
	Contributing time/money to worthy cause
	Involving family in community-based activities
	Establishing rules, structure, procedures for projects
	Proposing/implementing projects that affirm belief system
	Campaigning on behalf of candidate/important issue
	Mentoring a colleague, supervisee, or less experienced person
	Listing (and framing) "My Most Important Values"
	Displaying saying or idea supporting beliefs
	Sharing opinions with colleagues about what works well for you
	"Practicing what you preach"
	Being assertive about your limits
	Writing a letter to the editor

	Imaginer
Character Strengths:	*Imaginative, reflective, calm*
Perceptual Preferences:	Reflections; inactions
Motivating Factors:	Solitude; personal space
Distress Patterns:	
First Degree:	Needs to be strong
Second Degree:	Appears embarrassed; is shy; withdraws
Needs Fulfillment:	Spending alone time
	Volunteering for projects to be done alone
	Meditating
	Taking up solitary pursuits—cycling, walking, etc.
	Taking vacations alone
	Collecting coins, stamps, etc.
	Closing the office door when things are too active
	Using noise-canceling headphones
	Reading
	Receiving clear directions, then being left alone
	Having office/work place out of the mainstream
	Collecting data/doing "quiet" research (library, etc.)
	Establishing routines for repetitive tasks
	Setting limits for interaction, then withdrawing if they are exceeded

	Rebel
Character Strengths:	Spontaneous, creative, playful
Perceptual Preferences:	Reactions (likes and dislikes)
Motivating Factors:	Contact, fun activities
Distress Patterns:	
First Degree:	Tries hard; feigns lack of understanding/inability
Second Degree:	Blames others; acts irresponsibly; invites negative sanctions
Needs Fulfillment:	Having a good sense of humor
	Telling jokes and amusing anecdotes
	Using word play and puns
	Playing *before* work
	Reacting with excitement: "Wow!" "C-ooo-l!"
	Playing a musical instrument
	Writing music or short stories or plays
	Painting, sculpting, or other artistic outlets
	Decorating with exciting colors and stimulating things
	Being active in sports that are fun
	Staying involved in projects with "buddies"
	Dressing for the "mood"
	Using a personal listening device (MP3 player, iPod, mobile phone, etc.) while working or exercising
	Taking a play break at work—video/computer games, etc.
	Looking for creative solutions to knotty problems
	Acting in community theater
	"Coloring outside the lines"

	Promoter
Character Strengths:	*Adaptable, persuasive, charming*
Perceptual Preferences:	Actions
Motivating Factors:	Incidence; excitement
Distress Patterns:	
First Degree:	Wants others to be strong or fend for themselves
Second Degree:	Attempts to manipulate people or situations; breaks rules; tries to instigate conflict between others
Needs Fulfillment:	Having lots of things going on
	Being involved in projects/tasks with quick rewards/payoffs
	Competing positively
	Being involved in physical or kinesthetic things
	Getting to the "bottom line"
	Getting involved in exciting projects
	Negotiating "perks" for tasks completed well before deadlines
	Traveling for professional business as often as possible
	Riding the big rides at the fair/amusement park
	"Playing" the stock market (within monetary constraints)
	Driving a "fun" car—convertible, "red," etc.
	Dressing to impress others (again, within budgetary limits)

Appendix B
Dealing with Distress: Suggestions for Responses to Behaviors

This sections suggests how a leader might deal with the distress that occurs when motivational needs are not met. The lack of need fulfillment shows up in the symptoms listed below.

- *Withdraws*: This is the second-degree distress you will see from someone in Imaginer phase, being driven by "I have to be strong to be OK." Most likely she is not getting her *solitude* need met.

    An initial response might be, *"Dorothy, you have been asked to do a lot of things. Take this afternoon off and do something for yourself."*
    Other things you can do:
    ◦ Give her clear directions, then leave her alone
    ◦ Give her an office/work place out of the mainstream
    ◦ Assign her data collecting/doing "quiet" research (library, etc.)
    ◦ Establish routines for her to do repetitive tasks

- *Overcontrols*: This is the second-degree distress you will see from someone in Thinker phase, being driven by "I have to be perfect to be OK." Most likely he is not getting his *recognition for work* or *time structure* needs met.

    An initial response might be, *"Alfred, you do good work. How long do you think it will take you to come up with options to deal with the problem we are facing? What do you see the alternatives to be?"*
    Other things you can do:
    ◦ Set priorities for projects
    ◦ Focus on doing what is most important
    ◦ Arrange for acknowledgment of his accomplishments
    ◦ Set clear times frames and responsibilities

- Assign him tasks with tangible outcomes of completion
- Invite him to attending workshops to increase his skills or expertise/data base

• *Becomes vindictive*: This is the second-degree distress you will see from someone in Promoter phase, being driven by "you have to be strong to be OK." Most likely he is not getting his *incidence* need met.

An initial response might be, "Doug, tell me what you see the bottom line to be and how long it will take to get there." (Again, it is unlikely you will see many people with strong Promoter energy. They will choose other avenues or set themselves up to be eliminated.)

Other things you can do:
- Involve him in projects/tasks with quick rewards/payoffs
- Allow him to compete positively with co-workers
- Involve him in physical/kinesthetic things
- Direct him to get to the "bottom line" as quickly as he needs
- Involve him in exciting projects
- Let him understand the "perks" for assigned tasks well before deadlines
- When appropriate, have him travel on professional business as often as possible

• *Preaches*: This is the second-degree distress you will see from someone in Persister phase, being driven by "you have to be perfect to be OK." Most likely he is not getting his *recognition for work* or *conviction* needs met.

An initial response might be, "Matthew, you are an important member of our staff. Your contributions are valuable. Your perspective contributes to our seeing a full picture of our direction."

Other things you might do:
- Share your personal values and beliefs
- Ask him to establish rules, structure, procedures for projects
- Assign him the proposing/implementing projects that affirm his belief system
- Ask him to mentor a colleague or less experienced person

• *Blames*: This is the second-degree distress you will see from someone in Rebel phase, being driven by "I have to be try hard to be OK." Most likely she is not getting her *playful contact* need met.

An initial response might be, "Angie, I like the great enthusiasm and fresh approaches you bring to our staff. Wow! I am glad we have your energy to help us."

Other things you might do:
- Joke with her
- Tell her jokes and amusing anecdotes
- Use word play and puns with her
- Allow her to play *before* working

- *Invites criticism*: This is the second-degree distress you will see from someone in Harmonizer phase, being driven by "I have to please you to be OK." Most likely she is not getting her *acceptance of self* or *sensory* needs met.

  An initial response might be, "Barbara, you are so caring. The warmth you bring to our staff allows us to be comfortable in difficult situations—and even when things are not difficult. Thank you."
  Other things you might do:
  - Allow her to create her own "nest" at work
  - Arrange to recognize and accept her as a person
  - Assign her to lead and work with groups of people who appreciate her
  - Assign her to work on projects that help others

(Adapted with permission from Kahler, T. [1996]. *The advanced Process Communication seminar.* Little Rock, AR: Kahler Communications, Inc.)

About the Author

Michael Gilbert, EdD, is CEO of ATOIRE Communications, LLC, and professor emeritus in educational leadership at Central Michigan University. He has been involved with the preparation of educational and other leaders since 1975. He may be contacted at atoirecomm@gmail.com.

www.ingramcontent.com/pod-product-compliance
Lightning Source LLC
Chambersburg PA
CBHW071832230426
43672CB00013B/2822